Earthquake Ready

EARTHQUAKE READY

The Complete Preparedness Guide
Revised Edition

Virginia Kimball

Technical Advisor
Kate Hutton
Staff Seismologist,
California Institute of Technology

Illustrations by John Kimball

Roundtable Publishing, Inc.
Malibu, California

ROUNDTABLE PUBLISHING, INC.
29169 Heathercliff
Malibu, CA 90265

For my daughters, Katherine and Sarah

First Printing, 1988
Revised Edition, First Printing 1992

Library of Congress Cataloging-in-Publication Data

Kimball, Virginia.
  Earthquake ready / Virginia Kimball ; technical advisor,
Kate Hutton ; illustrations by John Kimball. — 3rd ed.
    p. cm.
  Includes bibliographical references (p.240) and index.
  ISBN 0-915677-60-1 :
  1. Earthquakes. 2. Earthquake preparedness. 3. Disaster
response. 4. Earthquake prediction. I. Title.
QE539.K55 1992   91-16222
363.3′495—dc20   CIP

9 8 7 6 5 4 3 2 1

PRINTED IN THE UNITED STATES OF AMERICA

Acknowledgments

I don't have all the answers, and I can't offer any guarantees. However, there is some good advice that I can offer, based on research, talking to experts, and personal experience. What will happen to any one person in an earthquake is completely unpredictable, but there is solid evidence of what will work for most people. Earthquakes are survivable. Knowing what to do and planning in advance will make them even more survivable, while enhancing the quality of survival.

In hopes of saving lives and preventing injury, damage, misunderstanding, and panic, many people have contributed to the revised edition of this book. I am particularly grateful to Kate Hutton, who read and corrected my manuscript, patiently answering countless questions, and to my literary agent, Mike Hamilburg. I would also like to thank the following friends and experts who gave generously of their time and expertise:

Peggy Brutsche, Education Coordinator, American Red Cross, Northern California Earthquake Relief and Preparedness Project
Pat Snyder, Volunteer Consultant, American Red Cross
Bill Gates, Dames and Moore Civil Engineers
Larry Ehrmann, Emergency Preparedness Coordinator, Department of Public Works, City of Los Angeles
Henry Johnson, Fire & Safety Specialist, Los Angeles City Fire Department
Jim Goltz, Geologist, Southern California Earthquake Preparedness Project (SCEPP)

Carl A. von Hake, Cooperative Institute for Research in Environmental Sciences (CIRES), University of Colorado/NOAA

Carl Stover, United States Geological Survey

Peter L. Ward, United States Geological Survey

Frank G. Diegmann, D.V.M., The Cat Clinic

Richard L. Shackelford, D.V.M., Teresita Animal Hospital

Paul Jennings, Ph.D., Chairman, Division of Engineering and Applied Science, CalTech

Bonnie Sloan, American Red Cross

Katherine Breen, Western Insurance Information Service

Michael G. Manfro, Safety and Environmental Affairs Manager, *Los Angeles Times*

Marty Beeman, PhD, LCSW, Senior Care Network, Huntington Memorial Hospital, Pasadena

Rich Eisner, Director, Bay Area Regional Earthquake Preparedness Project

Contents

PART IV
EARTHQUAKE PREDICTION
AND FUTURE PLANNING

APPENDICES

Foreword

The big question in the public mind with regard to earthquakes seems to be: "Will it happen?" And the answer is, of course, "Yes." If you live on the West Coast of the United States or in Alaska, you live in a place that has been "earthquake country" for millions of years and shows every sign of continuing to be in the future. You have already had, within this century, more than one sample of nature at its most violent—San Francisco, 1906, and Anchorage, 1964. In addition, there have been numerous somewhat smaller, but still damaging and frightening, earthquakes—San Fernando, 1971; Imperial Valley, 1979; Livermore, 1980; Whittier Narrows, 1987; and Loma Prieta, 1989.

The current "best guess," from Kerry Sieh's work at Pallett Creek, for example, indicates that southern California should experience a "great" (Magnitude 7.5 or larger) earthquake once every 140 years, give or take 30 years. Since the last one occurred in 1857 (135 years ago), we do not appear to be overdue, but we are approaching that time when we need to take the problem very seriously. Greater Los Angeles and San Bernardino have grown immensely in both size and complexity since 1857. Obscure accounts from the area, as it was more than a century ago, do not begin to prepare us for the scale of the disaster that could happen this time. A recent federal report on California's state of readiness estimates that anywhere from 3,000 to 13,000 persons might be killed, and roughly four times that number injured. In all probability, a recurrence interval of the same order applies to northern

California as well, with the last great earthquake having been in 1906.

In the same area, southern California, M6.0 and greater earthquakes are roughly fifty times more common than the great ones. Such an event can cause serious damage, although usually only in a limited area. Nevertheless, it has been estimated that an earthquake in the M7.0 range, if it occurred directly under downtown Los Angeles, could be more damaging and more deadly than a M8.0 event on the San Andreas.

On the other hand, California's public and political awareness of the earthquake hazard has made it one of the safest of seismic areas in the world. Seismic design requirements of one sort or another have been in the building code for more than half a century. The most prevalent type of construction for housing, namely wood-frame and stucco, is both strong and lightweight. In recent years, many southern California cities have taken positive steps to reinforce or remove the worst of the old unreinforced masonry structures. Earthquakes of the size that only rattle our nerves (around M5.0 or so) routinely take lives in many other parts of the world.

Another hopeful development in the past decade or so has been the discovery of measurable earthquake precursors, or phenomena that may indicate that an earthquake is about to happen. They are very poorly understood at present, and some earthquakes may not have them at all, but they do open a door to the possibility of earthquake prediction.

The state, local, and federal governments appear to be doing a fair job of "gearing up" for earthquake predictions. This is a difficult thing for them to do, because scientists are very seldom confident enough about an earthquake prediction to give a probability of occurrence much higher than about ten percent. In other words, they still expect most of their predictions to be wrong. Improvements may be expected in the future, but it may be unrealistic to expect earthquake predictors to ever be much better than weather predictors are now.

However, there are conceivable situations where seismologists would become very worried. Governments and individual citizens must be prepared to deal with the prediction of a serious earthquake as well as the earthquake itself. In November of 1987, a M6.0 earthquake occurred on a fault now known as the Elmore Ranch fault, which cuts across the northern part of the Imperial Valley. Aftershocks of this event were occurring within a few miles of the end of the locked part of the San Andreas fault. Scientists predictably became concerned, and a meeting of CEPEC, the California Earthquake Prediction Evaluation Council, was convened by teleconference. CEPEC felt that no public announcement was warranted. Even though the chances of a large earthquake on the San Andreas in the following few days were unquestionably much higher than they are normally, the odds were still thought to be fairly low. Perhaps if there had been accelerated creep of the San Andreas, rapidly changing water levels in wells, and more animal behavior reports than anyone knew what to do with, the situation might have been different. CEPEC did meet, however, in a crisis situation, and similar situations are likely to arise in the future. It turns out that there was a larger earthquake the next day, a M6.6, but it was on the Superstition Hills fault rather than the San Andreas.

There are appropriate measures for governments to take in the face of even low probability earthquakes predictions. Emergency personnel could be alerted, fire trucks could be parked outside, generators could be tested, and so forth. The same is true for the individual citizen. Such a time might be a good one to rotate the emergency food and water supply, if that has not already been done, check the flashlights and fire extinguishers, make sure that all family members recall the emergency plan. If the expected earthquake does not occur, then you can simply be relieved and confident that you are prepared. If it does occur, then you would have been prepared.

Meanwhile, most earthquakes are still taking seismologists and everyone else by surprise. We cannot count on getting any warning of an earthquake. And we cannot wait for a warning before making basic preparations.

The ostrich attitude is unrealistic in earthquake-prone regions, since an earthquake, perhaps a disastrous one, could happen to you. On the other hand, even a great earthquake does not imply certain death. There are many measures that you can take to improve your chances of survival and reduce your property loss. *Earthquake Ready* will show you how.

Kate Hutton
Staff Seismologist
California Institute of Technology
Pasadena, California

Introduction

It could happen at any moment. While you're eating breakfast . . . climbing steps to your seat at a football game . . . pushing a cart through the supermarket . . . riding an elevator up twenty stories . . . retrieving your car from a parking structure . . . asleep in bed. You hear a rumbling sound and catch your breath, as the ground beneath you starts to move. The possibilities race through your mind: an explosion . . . a bomb . . . an earthquake. The shaking continues, and you know what it is. It should stop now, but it doesn't. Whatever was on your mind isn't there now. Your only thought is survival. What can you do to shield yourself from the debris falling all around you? What if the structure above or below you collapses? How are you going to get out? Why didn't you think of this before?

It was dawn, February 9, 1971, when the San Fernando earthquake awakened my husband and me. The roaring noise arrived first, followed by the waves of motion that tossed us into the air, while our bed slid back and forth across the room. It was as though a fairy-tale giant had taken hold of our house and was shaking it, punishing us for unknown transgressions. Popping sounds, shattering glass, flashes of light, the crashing and slamming of our possessions being bounced this way and that, and our own involuntary screams brought us to the reality of an earthquake—a "moderate" earthquake.

Figure I-1. Rescuers dig through rubble at the site of the collapsed San Fernando Veterans Administration Hospital, where forty-four people were killed as a result of the 1971 earthquake. (Photo courtesy Los Angeles Department of Building and Safety.)

Afterwards, we rushed outside with our baby, and sat on our front lawn in Sylmar, a suburb of Los Angeles, in the San Fernando Valley. An eerie silence filled the air. All the normal sounds of our machine-based city were gone. Gradually the neighbors appeared, calling to one another to ask if anyone was hurt. The ground continued to shake from time to time. We waited, allowing our nerves and the ground to calm down.

In the foothills above us, clouds of dust were rising, caused, as we later discovered, by landslides and the collapse of the San Fernando Veterans Administration Hospital about a mile away. There were no injuries in our neighborhood, and we could see no buildings that had collapsed, although some houses had suffered structural damage, and all had interior damage. Our telephone didn't work, nor did the gas, electricity, or running water. We finally turned to the clean-up job awaiting us on the floors of our house, running to a doorway for shelter with each aftershock.

Up the hill, at the Veterans Hospital, four hours passed before outside authorities were informed that the old hospital building had collapsed and that people were buried—some alive, some dead. In the confusion following the earthquake, a police officer was told of the catastrophe. When he called in the report to headquarters, the hospital was mistakenly identified as the Olive View Hospital, a new Veterans Administration facility nearby, which had also suffered severe damage. A helicopter pilot surveying the area hours later reported the San Fernando Veterans Hospital collapse, and rescue operations were at last officially begun. The bodies of forty-four people were recovered from the demolished building.

Reflecting on these experiences, I realize how lucky we were to have been at home in bed when the earthquake struck and to have escaped unhurt. John and I were not prepared for an earthquake, and we could have been. We are both native Californians, had experienced earthquakes before, and shared an interest in geology and physical geography. Yet we, like most of those around us, were caught almost completely unprepared.

Fortunately, we had selected the most earthquake-resistant of homes, a single-story wood frame stucco house on a slab foundation. We hadn't consciously selected it for its earthquake-resistance, although we would have rejected a stone or brick house for the lack of it. That was just about the extent of our earthquake awareness: stone houses can collapse during earthquakes. We wouldn't have chosen a home too close to a major fault, either. The fault that was responsible for the San Fernando earthquake was considered to be inactive.

The inside of our home was not at all prepared for an earthquake. Many personal treasures were thrown to the floor and broken. At the time, we were so happy that our family was safe, that we didn't mourn the loss of physical

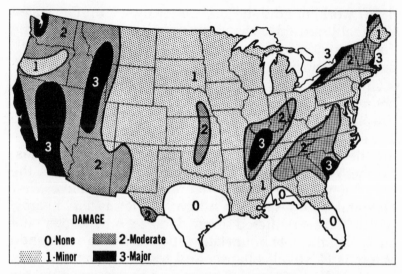

Figure I-2. Seismic risk map for the United States, not including Alaska and Hawaii, identifies four zones: Zone 0, areas with no reasonable expectancy of earthquake damage; Zone 1, expected minor damage; Zone 2, expected moderate damage; and Zone 3, where major destructive earthquakes may occur. (Map courtesy ESSA/Coast and Geodetic Survey.)

objects, replaceable or not. We repaired or replaced the essentials, and simply did without the china and crystal wedding gifts and other special losses. Our family was safe and our expected baby was born six months later, healthy and normal, and these were the things that mattered. But we shouldn't have had to rely on luck alone.

When we moved into our home in Sylmar, I gave no thought to earthquakes as I unpacked. Consciously or not, I had the idea of fire safety in my mind, as I arranged the furnishings. Now that we have children, their safety is always in the back of our minds, and we plan for safety out of habit. We don't surround ourselves with known fire hazards that we can avoid; we don't cross the street in front of moving trucks, or strike a match while filling our gas tanks. Why, then, should we live with earthquake hazards?

We can't eliminate earthquakes, but we can take action to protect lives and property from some of their destructive fury. We can also make preparations to meet the challenges of the moments, hours, and days following a disaster. Our homes can be made safer and we can learn to identify potential earthquake hazards—such as unsafe buildings, slide areas, old weakened bridges, and other dangerous structures—so that we can make informed choices about the risks we take. The places where we work can be evaluated for earthquake safety, and we can supply our desks or lockers with emergency supplies, such as flashlights, to assist after a disaster.

Don't assume that only California and Alaska have earthquakes. While it's true that in the United States there are many more earthquakes along the West Coast, earthquakes can and do happen in every state. Since 1700, more than a thousand earthquakes have been reported east of the Mississippi River. Earthquakes that caused widespread and severe damage have occurred in Charleston, South Carolina (1886-87), New Madrid, Missouri (1811), Hebgen Lake, Montana (1959), and Borah Peak, Idaho (1983). The map of earthquake risk in the United States shows that there are very few areas in the United States that are considered low-risk for earthquakes. (See Appendix for maps of earthquake locations in the United States.)

Wherever you live, being prepared for an earthquake makes good sense. And many of the preparations outlined here—such as assembling an earthquake kit, knowing how to shut off major utilities, and having an evacuation plan—would be useful in other emergency situations as well. Earthquakes will continue to happen, sometimes causing death and destruction, but being prepared will make the difference.

Part I

The Earthquake

Part I

1

What Happens During An Earthquake

THE SUDDEN SHOCK

Small earthquakes may seem like fun. Just about the time you begin to feel a little shaking and start to wonder, "Is this an earthquake?" the shaking stops. You may have to wait for the TV or radio news to find out if it really was an earthquake or just a big truck rumbling by. If the hanging plants or lamps are swaying, it probably was an earthquake. Minor shakes such as these, and many which are even less noticeable, are the most common type, occurring daily in many places. Although these small earth movements are rarely felt, and do no appreciable damage, the ones we do feel serve to remind us that the earth is in a state of constant change and that the forces of nature are beyond our control.

Slightly bigger quakes usually give you time to recognize their presence, but in about the time it takes to move under a desk, the shaking stops. Dishes and window panes will rattle as the ground shakes, and glasses perched on the edge of a table may fall and break, but the disturbance in an earthquake of this size is usually confined to people's nerves.

Moderate and great earthquakes shake the ground hard enough to cause a lot of action. The extent of damage depends on how hard and for how long the ground is shaking. The motion may be erratic—from side to side as well as up and down. Strong shaking can last from fifteen to forty seconds or more, occasionally more than a minute, but will invariably seem to last much longer.

The main shock may be followed closely by a series of aftershocks, which are smaller than the main shock and generally decrease in size and frequency. Earthquakes don't follow rules, though. Some are preceded by smaller quakes, called foreshocks. Others strike with no apparent warning. Sometimes earthquakes occur in clusters or swarms, groups of shocks that are roughly the same size.

If there were a typical moderate earthquake, it would be preceded by a few small foreshocks that at the time may have seemed insignificant. It is only by looking back at a sequence of earthquakes that the foreshocks can be identified as such. The main shock would then be followed by a series of progressively smaller and less frequent aftershocks.

Some great earthquakes in the recorded past have not followed typical patterns. The great Chilean quake of 1960 was preceded by a large shock, a series of smaller ones, and then, the next day, by two sharp foreshocks that struck just before the great earthquake. At M9.5, this was the strongest earthquake of this century to date. Many more people would have died if the buildings had not been evacuated following the earlier quakes.

An earthquake arrives in a series of shock waves of different velocity. There may be loud thumping rhythms and banging sounds with simultaneous shuddering vibrations. Sometimes people have reported hearing a roaring noise like a locomotive, or a low rumbling similar to thunder just before the shaking begins. This noise is probably the arrival of the earthquake activity itself: energy waves radiating through the crust of the earth that can be heard but not felt, as well as waves that travel a bit faster and precede the rest of the earthquake. Other sounds are caused by the earthquake's effects on the land and structures built upon it. Breaking glass, creaking boards, shivering or cracking trees, falling objects, landslides, sloshing water, collapsing walls, and crackling electricity all contribute to the incredible cacophony.

As the ground shakes, tall buildings sway. Weak or loose parts crack and fall. Inside, objects topple and fall from tables, desks, counters, and shelves. Pictures drop from the walls. The longer the shaking continues and the harder it shakes, the more dramatic the effects. Furniture tips over. Cupboard doors open and the contents crash to the floor. Windows crack or shatter. Ceilings and light fixtures fall. Mortar between bricks or rocks crumbles under the stress, allowing walls to collapse. Toppling appliances break their utility lines and gas begins to leak. Fires are ignited. Lights go out as the electrical lines are snapped. Elevators lurch to a stop between floors.

Outside, glass may be falling from windows overhead. Loose bricks, parapets, facades and signs may fall. Chimneys may collapse, usually breaking at the roofline and dropping bricks either at the base of the chimney or along a line outward from the base. Injuries could be caused by falling objects.

People can become disoriented and frightened. Most of what they see and feel is real, a nightmare wrenched to reality, but there may also be physiological effects that produce illusions, sights that appear real but are not. Some observers have reported seeing ripples or waves moving across solid surfaces, such as streets, pavement, or concrete floors during earthquakes. Sometimes cracks or soil disturbances are found afterwards. But in other cases, investigation after the earthquake does not reveal the kind of cracking which that type of action would have caused.

When people are hurt during earthquakes, the injuries are almost always caused by something that falls on them. If the shaking is strong enough, people may lose their balance and even be thrown to the ground, while trying to move to a safer place. It's not unusual for an earthquake to trigger a heart attack.

Facilities for the public such as dams, reservoirs, power plants, sewage treatment facilities, highways, bridges, tunnels, subways, auditoriums, stores, shopping centers, stadiums, and churches are all vulnerable to earthquake

Figure 1-1. The 1971 San Fernando earthquake created this scarp, uplifting a section of sidewalk and street. (Photo courtesy Los Angeles Department of Building and Safety.)

damage. Public services such as electricity, sewer lines, telephone lines, natural gas service, fire and police service, and hospitals may also be damaged. A great earthquake in a densely populated area will usually cause widespread damage and injury. Even a small to moderate quake, with its epicenter in or near a city, may cause massive destruction.

The time of day that an earthquake strikes a populated area plays a large part in determining the number of casualties. Although many earthquakes have struck while people were home in bed, they could just as easily occur during morning or evening rush-hour traffic, or during business or recreational hours when many people are at amusement parks, ball games, beaches, and movies. An earthquake can occur at any time of day or night.

LAND SHIFTS AND WATER CHANGES

Scarps.

Sections of ground may be elevated or subside during earthquakes. Sometimes one side of a fault will rise or sink, creating a scarp (an earthquake-caused cliff) where the ground's surface had originally been intact. Scarps may be lifted again and again in successive earthquakes, with the uplift in any one earthquake ranging from fractions of an inch to several feet or more. The vertical uplifting may be combined with horizontal movement as well, or the fault movement may be primarily horizontal.

Slides.

Unstable hillsides may slump or slide during or after the shaking. Rocks may break loose and slide down hillsides, sometimes creating rock avalanches. If snow and ice are present, a snow avalanche can occur, sometimes combining with rocks or mud to cause even greater damage. The underground water system may also be disturbed by an earthquake, causing fluctuations in water pressure and stream volume, and the appearance or disappearance of springs. Well water levels or temperature can change, and the water can become cloudy or muddy. Underground oil and gas deposits could be similarly disturbed.

Tsunamis.

An earthquake undersea or near the coastline strong enough to rock the sea floor and disturb the mass of water over it, could cause a series of huge waves known as tsunamis—seismic sea waves, or less precisely, tidal waves. The term "tidal wave" probably came about because the first large wave in the series is preceded by a trough or depression resembling an extremely low tide. As the wave approaches shore, the water line pulls back, sometimes revealing interesting sights on the bottom of the sea, which can attract unwary observers. Soon afterwards, the first wave hits, pulls back again, and is followed by another. There may be a dozen or more great waves in the sequence, or possibly only a few. Tsunamis can be generated by a variety of seismic events and land movements including: volcanic explosions and landslides, undersea or into the sea, and of course, by earthquakes.

In the same way as a series of waves will radiate from the impact of a pebble thrown into a pond, tsunamis move outwardly over the ocean from the seismic focal point. The irregular sea floor and coastline can either dissipate or funnel the waves. A tsunami may devastate one beach, while leaving a neighboring area untouched. Because of their depth, shape, and/or orientation, some harbors, such as the one at Crescent City, California, can amplify the power of a tsunami, while others will not. The waves

Figure 1-2. This photograph was taken during a landslide caused by an aftershock following the 1971 San Fernando earthquake. (Photo by Mavis Shafer.)

*Figure 1-3. A rockslide caused by the earthquake of July 9, 1958, gener-
ated a wave at Lituya Bay, Alaska, that surged 1,720 feet up the
mountainside, destroying forest in the light areas. (Photo courtesy
NOAA/EDS.)*

travel about four hundred miles per hour. Because of the
long distance from crest to crest, they would not be
noticed by seafaring vessels and pose no threat to them.
As the waves approach land, they gain in height and
reveal their destructive potential. A worldwide warning
system exists so that people threatened by a tsunami will
usually be alerted in time to evacuate; however, there may
not be time to issue a warning for the area immediately
affected by the seismic event that generates such a wave.

Seiches.

When an enclosed body of water such as a bay, a lake,
a swimming pool, or even a pan of water is rocked, the
water may begin to slosh back and forth rhythmically.
During this phenomenon, known as a "seiche," the water
surges from one side to the other, often gaining in

Figure 1-4. Tsunami damage in Kodiak, Alaska, caused by the earthquake of March 27, 1964. (Photo courtesy NOAA/EDS.)

Figure 1-5. State Highway 287 disappeared into Montana's Hebgen Lake during the earthquake of August 18, 1959, creating a large seiche. (Photo courtesy NOAA/EDS.)

intensity, and may overflow its basin before gradually slowing down and stopping. In the 1959 Hebgen Lake, Montana, earthquake, an exceptionally large seiche caused three waves to overflow the dam, and the water continued to oscillate for ten hours. Seiches have been observed even thousands of miles from a great earthquake.

Liquefaction.

Loose soils with a high water table (water in the soil close to the surface) may experience the phenomenon of liquefaction. As the earthquake causes water to percolate up through the loose soil, it becomes like quicksand. Heavy objects such as buildings and other structures may sink or tilt into the liquefied soil. Hillsides or earth-filled dams situated over such an area could also collapse. The effect is temporary, but the results can be very damaging. Much of the non-fire damage in San Francisco in the 1906 and 1989 earthquakes was caused by liquefaction of the water-saturated soil along the Bay. The thick alluvium at the upper end of the great Mississippi River Delta is particularly susceptible to liquefaction. A series of earthquakes occurring near New Madrid, Missouri, on December 16, 1811, January 23, 1812, and February 7, 1812 caused widespread damage due to liquefaction and other problems associated with alluvial soils.

THE EARTH'S SHIFTING CRUST

What we feel as an earthquake results from the sudden release of energy when pieces of the earth's crust move against one another. Early observers thought that the shaking of the earth caused sections of rock or land to move, but scientists now know that the reverse is true; the moving of great pieces of earth causes the shaking.

By observing earthquake energy waves traveling through the earth, scientists are developing a better understanding of the earth's composition. The earth is

Figure 1-6. Liquefaction allowed this building to sink and tip onto its side during the earthquake of June 16, 1964, in Niigata, Japan. (Photo courtesy NOAA/EDS.)

composed of rock that becomes increasingly dense and hot toward the center. The core is extremely dense liquid, probably nickel and iron. Between the core and the surface of the earth lies the mantle, composed of molten rock so hot that it is in a pliable state. The cooled, hardened crust is about twenty miles thick and is fractured into huge plates, which are constantly shifting position and changing as the crust renews itself.

Plate Tectonics.

The movement of the massive plates was first recognized as continental drift, part of a controversial theory first put forth by Alfred Wegener, a German meteorologist and astronomer, in 1910. His idea that the present continents were once joined as one huge continent that later drifted apart, was greeted with widespread ridicule and condemnation. Although a growing number of scientists during the thirties followed up on Wegener's work, it was not until the period following World War II that confirmation of his theory was found. Stripes of opposing magnetism were discovered on the ocean floor emanating from ocean ridges, which we now know to be the boundaries of oceanic plates.

During the past twenty years, the theory of "plate tectonics" has become widely accepted as the basis of a new comprehension of the earth. We now understand that the earth's crust is broken into tectonic plates, like pieces of an enormous jigsaw puzzle molded around a sphere—stretching, tilting, bulging, and cracking in an ongoing process of change. This continuing process has been going on for millions of years, long before human beings became aware of the dramatic consequences of plate movement.

As the plates move apart, which usually happens under oceans, magma oozes upward to fill the gaps and enable the crust to renew itself. Submarine ridges are created as the magma wells up and solidifies. This new rock continues to cool, increases in density, and acquires its magnetic orientation, as it becomes part of the sea floor. Exciting new discoveries along these submarine ridges include vents with hot, mineral-rich water squirting out of "chimneys," and colonies of strange new life forms thriving on chemicals in the heated sea water.

Other edges of the plates are being forced downward, under other plates, to be broken up, reheated, and reabsorbed into the magma as part of the earth's gradual recycling of the crust. In the twentieth century, this is happening beneath the Cascade Mountains in Washington, Oregon, and northern California, and along the Chilean Coast. Volcanic activity is frequently generated on the overriding plate, along a line about one-hundred kilometers from the edge. These slow collisions of the great plates are now believed to have been responsible for the formation of most of the world's mountain ranges. The massive 1960 earthquake in Chile, which triggered tsunamis, rock slides, flooding, and some volcanic activity, was caused by the elastic strain deep under the coast, as the oceanic plate plunged under the continental plate.

Other plates are sliding past one another. Sometimes they get stuck and build up tension until they snap free. This type of plate movement caused the great San Francisco earthquake of 1906. The San Andreas Fault marks the boundary between the Pacific Plate and the North American Plate. In the famous San Francisco earthquake, the Pacific Plate, moving in a northwesterly direction, and the North American Plate, moving toward the west, were trying to move past one another. Instead, they locked together, built up stress, and finally broke free, releasing energy along a 225 mile stretch, most disastrously in the San Francisco Bay area, where the Pacific Plate may have moved as much as twenty-one feet to the northwest.

Volcanic Activity.

Along the edges of the Pacific Ocean, the boundary of the Pacific Plate is marked by a wide zone of spectacular geologic activity. The belt from New Zealand, up through Japan, rounding the Aleutian Islands, up to Alaska, and down the coasts of North and South America, is known as the "ring of fire." Located here are almost two-thirds of the world's active volcanoes and a history of many of the world's great earthquakes. In those dynamic areas along the boundaries between plates, and occasionally in other "hot spots"—Hawaii and Iceland, for example— magma sometimes moves upward, lifting and bursting through the crust, forming volcanoes.

Activity under or inside volcanoes, particularly the movement of magma, sometimes causes earthquakes. These volcanic earthquakes are different in that the shaking is generally limited to the immediate area of the volcano, and is usually of low magnitude. Harmonic tremors, a particular type of earth movement detectable on seismographs, are caused by the upward movement of magma within a volcano.

Volcanoes can produce spectacular displays of power, but earthquakes are not the most dangerous aspect of these. The huge explosion of Mount St. Helens, Washington, on May 18, 1980, sent about a cubic mile of pulverized rock and ash fourteen miles into the air, and devastated the surrounding area by the force of the blast accompanied by superheated steam, ash, and gases, but its earthquakes were generally minor. Most of them were below M4.0 and the greatest, which occurred just before the volcanic explosion, measured M5.1. People who are close enough to active volcanoes to feel the earthquakes probably have much more to fear from other volcanic events such as explosions, gas, superheated clouds, mudflows, lava flows, smoke, and falling ash, dust, and pumice.

Faults.

The cracks in the earth's crust are called faults. They can be the dividing cracks between the plates, part of the fractured zones along some plate boundaries, or cracks anywhere in the earth's crust. A fault is not a hairline crack along the surface of the ground, but a zone or strip of ground where the earth's crust is broken by a vertical or nearly vertical crack. The great pressure and movement along the fault crumbles, cracks, and pulverizes the surrounding rock, creating a number of subsidiary faults which are called strands. Most major faults are complex zones made up of several strands. Movement, or slip, along these faults seems to occur repeatedly along one or a few of the multiple strands. The San Andreas Fault zone is considered to range in width from a few hundred feet to a mile. This massive fault is about six-hundred miles long, but it does not move as one unit. Different sections move at different rates. For example, during an earthquake, a southern section of the fault could be displaced by several feet, while the northern segment may not move at all.

Some areas, especially near plate boundaries, are crossed by a network of faults, and are called fracture zones. The Los Angeles area is such a zone. It is part of the Pacific Plate, located west of the San Andreas Fault. Although Los Angeles is definitely not on the verge of

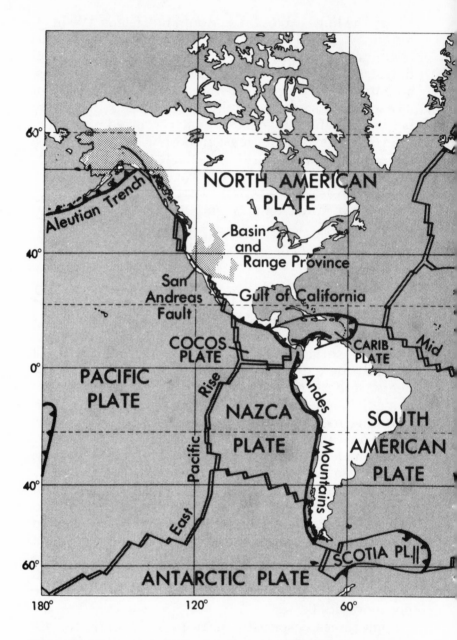

*Figure 1-7. The tectonic plates that form the earth's crust are identi-
fied with indications of their active boundaries. Double lines indicate plates moving apart. Lines with barbs indicate zones of
underthrusting where one plate is sliding beneath another; barbs*

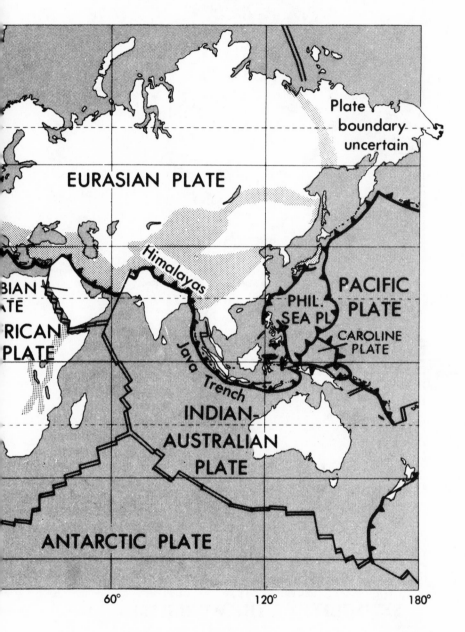

shown on overriding plate. Single lines indicate plates sliding past one another. Shaded areas on continents indicate areas other than boundaries that are undergoing active faulting. (Map courtesy United States Geological Survey.)

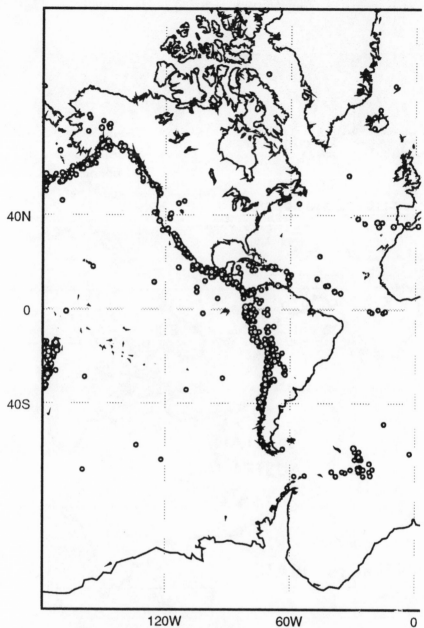

SEISMICITY OF THE WORLD   M >= 7.0

NATIONAL GEOPHYSICAL DATA CENTER /

Figure 1-8. Map of the world's great earthquakes (M8.0 and higher), 1897-1976. Note that great earthquakes occur

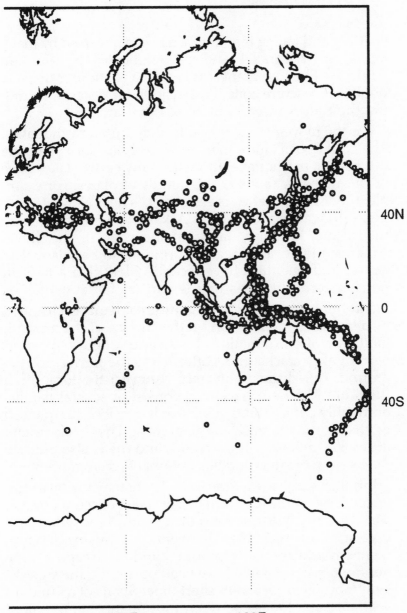

60E   120E

3170 EARTHQUAKES PLOTTED

NOAA BOULDER, CO 80303

primarily along plate boundaries. (Map courtesy United States Geological Survey.)

splitting and falling into the Pacific, it is traversed by many faults, both parallel and perpendicular to the San Andreas. The San Francisco Bay area is another densely populated fracture zone. Five major fault systems, including the San Andreas, cut across that area.

It is the movement along faults that causes earthquakes. The fault doesn't have to be near the boundary of a plate to cause an earthquake, though. Many earthquakes have been caused by faults in the middle of plates. For example, the 1811-1812 series of earthquakes near New Madrid, Missouri, caused damage in Arkansas, Tennessee, Kentucky, and Missouri, far from the edge of the North American Plate. That region continues to be seismically active, and scientists have recently identified a fault in northeastern Arkansas that is part of that system.

Although the presence of some great faults is indicated by a trough or depression on the surface of the ground, faults are often difficult to locate and identify. After an earthquake, cracks and patterns on the surface of the ground, called the "fault trace," suggest the location of the fault. The fault trace may consist of several parallel or roughly parallel lines or arcs, or it may look like plowed earth, or even the track of a giant mole. The displacement of streets, orchard rows, streams, and rivers also indicate the location of faults and the amount of recent movement.

But this is not always the case. There may not be a fault trace on the surface, or it may have been obscured by soft soils, the natural processes or erosion, landslides, and vegetation—or by human intervention. Housing developments, roadways, earth grading, and landscaping wipe out fault traces. People have been observing the signs of fault movement for a very short time. Spans of a hundred years or even longer between movements along a fault are not uncommon, and a hundred years ago most scientists felt that recording the location and measuring movement following earthquakes was not important, because they thought that the shaking caused the faulting. Today, geologists work from sketchy history and hidden evidence as they try to map our future earthquakes.

2

What Will Happen To You During An Earthquake?

What happens to you during an earthquake depends primarily on two factors: how big the earthquake is and where you are when it strikes. These two factors sound simple, but they are full of variables. Where you are, in particular, involves how close you are to the epicenter of the earthquake, what type of soil or rock is under you and what happens to it when it moves, how close you are to coastal and inland shores, the level of the ground water under you, the type of building you are in or near, its design and quality of construction, and the furnishings and other objects that surround you.

ELEMENTS OF TIME AND PLACE

The point where the earthquake begins, where the fault first moves, is called the *focus*. Different earthquakes have different depths of focus, meaning that they begin at different distances below the earth's surface. The point on the surface of the ground directly above the focus is called the *epicenter*. In general, the closer you are to the epicenter, the greater the effects of the earthquake on you.

Ground Movement.

Besides proximity to the epicenter and the size of the earthquake, the amount of shaking that occurs during an

27

earthquake is determined by the geologic makeup of the area. In general, bedrock will shake least, and loosely compacted soils—alluvium, sand, and landfill, for example—will shake more.

In addition to problems caused by the shaking itself, ground failure and ground displacement can also cause damage. The term *ground failure* refers to the inability of the ground to support whatever may be on it. Landslides, liquefaction, and uneven settling of soils are examples of ground failure. *Ground displacement* refers to sections of ground actually changing position either vertically, horizontally, or both. The amount of displacement is usually greatest along the main fault zone, and less along ruptures branching outward from it. If a building happens to be built right on top of a fault, it can suffer considerable damage as the ground under part of the foundation moves, and the rest does not.

Ground failure can be as inconsequential as a minor slide, or much more serious, as in Peru in 1970. On a bright Sunday afternoon in May, a large (M7.8) earthquake was felt near Chimbote, Peru. The jolting earth movements frightened people and knocked down some stone walls and houses, but there were few injuries and not too much immediate damage. Many people remained outside that day, enjoying the sunny weather, and milling about in the usual Sunday marketplace. Above them, however, high atop Mt. Huascaran, the earthquake broke loose a huge piece of rock and ice, which began a deadly journey down the steep slopes of the mountain. As it picked up speed, the icy avalanche increased in size by gathering rocks and other debris along its path.

Friction melted some of the ice, turning the soil under it into mud. Riding on what may have been a cushion of air at speeds up to two-hundred miles per hour, this crushing mass destroyed everything in its path including small towns, before finally crashing into the city of Yungay. The city, its fifteen-thousand residents, and an unknown number of visitors were killed, buried under

Figure 2-1. A massive landslide in Anchorage, Alaska, caused by the earthquake of March 27, 1964, damaged Fourth Avenue. (Photo courtesy NOAA/EDS.)

Figure 2-2. The garage walls of this home were inadequately braced for the heavy load they had to support. The upper level of the house ripped away, crushing the garage walls and the car inside. (Photo by Mavis Shafer.)

seventeen feet of debris. No accurate death toll was possible, but estimates ranged from thirty-thousand to
seventy-thousand fatalities. The same earthquake on level
bedrock might not have killed anyone.

Structural Factors.

Probably the greatest factor determining the extent of
damage to populated areas is the type and quality of construction. It has been observed for years that certain types
of houses endure earthquakes with little damage, while
other types frequently collapse. Houses built of adobe or
stone are particularly vulnerable to earthquake damage—
their weight serves to pull them apart during severe
shaking.

Wooden houses fare better, because they are lighter,
stronger, and more flexible. The single-story wood frame
house seems to withstand earthquakes very well. Sim-
plicity of design also improves earthquake resistance.
Square and rectangular box-like designs perform best in
earthquakes because they move as one unit, whereas
buildings with many wings and corners can twist and pull
apart under earthquake stresses. Building codes reflect
the growing body of knowledge of seismic engineering,
so modern buildings withstand earthquakes very well.

Other Complicating Hazards.

Earthquakes can also claim lives in buildings without
causing significant structural damage. Suspended ceilings, light fixtures, partitions, and windows could fall,
causing death or injury. Heavy furnishings such as bookcases and filing cabinets may also topple with disastrous
results.

One of the most dangerous byproducts of earthquakes
is fire. The great 1906 San Francisco earthquake was disastrous, but its tragic effects were multiplied by the fire
that raged for three days afterwards. An even greater
disaster struck Japan during the earthquake of September

Figure 2-3. This row of two-story buildings collapsed backward, away from the street, when the ground slumped beneath their foundations during the San Francisco earthquake of April 18, 1906. The photograph was taken before the fire destroyed the entire block. (Photo courtesy NOAA/EDS.)

1, 1923. It was just before noon in Tokyo and Yokohama when this devastating earthquake hit—a time when most Japanese families were preparing their midday meals inside their lightweight, earthquake-resistant homes. The toppling stoves ignited countless small fires in the houses, which joined together, created raging firestorms, claiming 143,000 lives.

A 1987 insurance industry study of the risk of fire following an earthquake indicated that both the Los Angeles area and the San Francisco Bay area face a serious risk of widespread conflagrations after an earthquake. The fire losses alone were estimated at fifteen-to-seventeen billion dollars. These figures do not include earthquake-related lawsuits, business interruption, damage to vehicles, and damage caused by earthquake shaking.

One of the greatest fire dangers in the United States is to an occupied high-rise building such as the November,

1980 fire at the MGM Grand Hotel in Las Vegas or the May, 1988 fire in the First Interstate Bank Tower in Los Angeles. Although these disasters were not earthquake-related, similar fires could be ignited by an earthquake. To complicate matters, water supplies for fire fighting, communication networks, and access to the building could be interrupted by the earthquake, hampering emergency response to a high-rise fire.

Similar problems might make it equally difficult to fight any large fire after an earthquake, particularly if it were to occur during dry, windy weather such as Los Angeles' Santa Ana winds. Other weather conditions during an earthquake can often exacerbate its destructive power. Freezing temperatures, snow storms, or saturated hillsides during or after a heavy rain could provide a frightening addition to an earthquake.

Dams are a particular source of concern during an earthquake. Eighty-thousand people were evacuated due to the threatened collapse of the Van Norman Dam in the 1971 San Fernando earthquake. Many of them didn't even know that the dam was there before it came so close to inundating them. Dikes and levees may also fail during earthquakes, causing flooding.

Dams are now being studied not only to see if they can withstand earthquakes, but interestingly, also to see if they may actually trigger them. The water that continually saturates the ground under a reservoir may serve to lubricate or weaken rock already under strain. Also, the weight of the large volume of water may place additional pressure on a fault, causing it to give way. There does seem to be a correlation between the depth of water behind high dams and the number of earthquakes in the immediate area.

One of the greatest hazards in populated areas is one which has been almost ignored, because it hasn't happened yet, and because its effects are almost unthinkable in their potential for devastation—earthquake-induced nuclear or chemical disaster. An earthquake could easily cause a nuclear accident or the release of toxic chemical products. Such damage could be initiated at nuclear and chemical facilities, as well as at various industrial plants and research facilities, which use and store hazardous materials, or by an accident involving the transportation of these materials.

Nuclear power plants located in areas with a history of seismic activity have been built under regulations designed to avoid earthquake damage, based on the largest earthquake expected in the area. Other facilities and the processes they use during their operation may not be protected from earthquake damage, and continue to pose a threat to the lives of the surrounding population.

Likewise, the transport of hazardous materials is dangerous, and accidents unrelated to earthquakes, especially train derailments, have occurred with increasing frequency in the United States. Ground shaking during an earthquake can tip over railroad cars or cause rail displacement and consequently the derailment of trains. If the train happens to be transporting hazardous cargo, the results could be disastrous. Similarly, earthquakes can cause truck and airport accidents, which could be equally serious. If such accidents should happen during a major earthquake, emergency help might be unavailable, unreachable, and inevitably delayed.

Time and Chance.

Where you will be during an earthquake may be as random as the chance selection of any moment in time. Who could have anticipated the fate of the drivers on the near-empty freeway at dawn who just happened to be under a freeway overpass bridge as it split and crashed to the ground during the 1971 San Fernando earthquake?

Survival is always a bit of a gamble, but the odds are that the earthquake will strike when you are in one of the places where you spend the most time. If you eliminate most of the hazards at home, work, and wherever you are most of the time, you will improve your chances of survival. How close you are to the epicenter

and to any of the environmental consequences of earthquakes will also help in determining your fate in such
an event. The other critical factor is the earthquake's size.

THE SIZE FACTOR: MEASURING THE QUAKE

Measuring the size of an earthquake can be approached
in two ways: by measuring the amount of energy released
by the earthquake (its magnitude), or by evaluating the
effects of the release of that energy upon objects and
geology (its intensity). The former is reported as a number usually ranging between 1 and 10 on the Richter scale
or some other magnitude scale, and the latter as a Roman
numeral from I (not felt) to XII (total damage) on the
Modified Mercalli Intensity scale.

Magnitude—The Richter Scale.

A seismograph records the ground motion at a particular location, usually as a squiggly line on a piece of paper
or as corresponding numbers on a computer. The peak
deflection, or "amplitude," caused by an earthquake is
used, along with the distance from the instrument to the
earthquake's epicenter and the characteristics of the
instrument itself, to compute its magnitude. The magnitude scale is a logarithmic scale, which means that each
whole number step on the scale represents an difference
of ten times in the size of the measured waves, and an
increase of about thirty times in the amount of energy
released by an earthquake.

For example, the San Fernando earthquake measured
M (for Magnitude) 6.4. An earthquake of M7.4 would
produce shock waves ten times as strong as the San Fernando quake. The 1906 San Francisco earthquake
occurred before Charles Richter devised his scale, but it
has been estimated as M8.3, which is nearly one-hundred
times stronger than the San Fernando earthquake. On
the average, the earth has ten major earthquakes (M7.0
to 7.9) and one great earthquake (M8.0 or larger) each year.

M2.0 is the smallest earthquake that is normally can be felt by human beings, and there are thousands of events of this size every day.

One confusing thing about the magnitude scale is that there are several versions of it, depending on what type of instrument was used for the determination and how far it was from the earthquake. The Richter scale, as originally formulated (usually referred to as "local magnitude" or M_L), is only reliable for earthquakes smaller than about 6.0. Larger events last longer, but do not generally produce any larger amplitude waves in the period range measured by the seismographs Richter used. The same is true for the so-called "body-wave magnitude" (M_b), which is estimated from similar short-period instruments that are at great distances.

For earthquakes larger than about 6.0, the "surface wave magnitude" (M_s) does better justice to the actual size of the earthquake. It is measured on long-period seismographs, generally at large distances from the epicenter. Even surface wave magnitude, however, does not properly account for the ultra-long-period energy released by the world's largest earthquakes.

Recently, seismologists have begun to use an ultra-long-period surface wave magnitude (M_w) and a seismic moment magnitude (M_o) for the largest earthquakes. The moment magnitude is probably the most reliable earthquake magnitude so far devised, but it is not as easy to calculate as the others so it is less commonly used. These more accurate measurements have led to revision of magnitudes for some of the more famous earthquakes. For example, the 1906 San Francisco earthquake is currently listed as $M_o7.9$, and the 1964 Alaska earthquake has "changed" to $M_o9.2$, making it the second largest earthquake in this century. The largest was the 1960 Chile earthquake, at $M_o9.5$.

Intensity—the Modified Mercalli Scale.

After an earthquake that causes damage, observations of the damage and accounts of personal experiences are

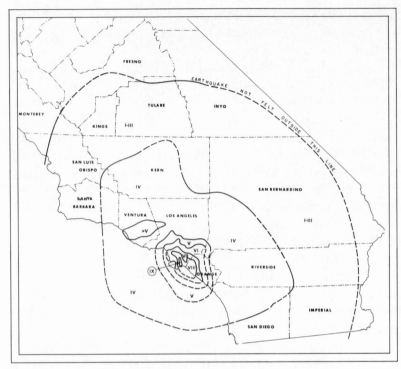

Figure 2-4. Intensity map of the 1933 Long Beach, California, earthquake. Zones are numbered to indicate the intensity with which the earthquake was felt, using the Modified Mercalli Scale of Intensity. (Map courtesy California Division of Mines and Geology.)

compiled and mapped to describe the earthquake's intensity. On the Modified Mercalli Scale, Roman numerals are assigned to describe the extent of ground shaking in different areas, based on observed effects on people, objects, and man-made structures. Where seismic instrument readings are not available or are incomplete, these direct observations fill in the gaps of information for seismologists. The U.S. Geological Survey, National Earthquake Information Center in Golden, Colorado mails questionnaires to postmasters and volunteer observers in earthquake areas, compiles the results by computer, then maps areas of varying intensity to provide a more complete picture for future study.

Part II

Planning For Survival

Planning for Success

3

Won't Science and Government Protect Us?

The government doesn't have special umbrellas that open automatically to protect citizens during a big earthquake. Civic agencies can't stop things from falling on top of people, which is how most of us are injured during earthquakes. Partial or total structure collapses, nonstructural hazards, and fires account for other earthquake injuries. Government regulations can prevent some of these problems, but individuals must do the rest.

The threat of an earthquake and its potentially disastrous aftermath of liability has forced government at all levels to make disaster plans. This advance planning could save lives, especially in the area of building safety. Despite plans, though, the minutes following a large earthquake will be chaotic.

With time, order will gradually come, as government agencies begin to respond. Personal planning is very important, and government planning, based on scientific research, is essential.

CONSTRUCTION ISSUES

Unreinforced Masonry.

The recognition of one great danger has contributed most to adding earthquake protection to buildings. The 1925 Santa Barbara and 1933 Long Beach, California, earthquakes revealed the hazards of unreinforced masonry construction, which includes buildings made of bricks, blocks, stones, with mortar, and without steel reinforcing. Banning new unreinforced masonry construction has made a great contribution to earthquake safety; however, eliminating this great danger doesn't mean that buildings constructed in other ways are necessarily safe.

Planning for Earthquake Resistance.

When the 1933 earthquake struck Long Beach, California, damage to buildings demonstrated the importance of proper design and construction. Many public buildings, especially schools, were heavily damaged. It was a moderate earthquake (M6.3), but it caused widespread damage that claimed 120 lives. Many buildings collapsed. Sidewalks and doorways in commercial areas were littered with fallen brick, concrete, and glass. People were horrified by the sight of schools with fallen roofs, collapsed walls, and rubble-strewn classrooms. The earthquake occurred at 5:54 p.m. Had it taken place a few hours earlier, when the schools were filled with children, casualties would have been very much higher.

As people had noticed eight years before in Santa Barbara, wooden buildings stood virtually undamaged next to collapsed brick buildings. It was clear that, although unreinforced masonry buildings did not perform well in earthquakes, buildings can be built to withstand the shaking. Scandals followed the discovery of poor workmanship and deficient materials used in constructing the schools. The California legislature responded to the public outrage by passing the Field Act, which required new schools to be built earthquake resistant. Forty years would pass before all California public schools, new and old, finally met seismic safety standards. But at least the idea of planning for earthquake resistance in buildings was beginning to take hold.

The year of the Long Beach earthquake is considered to be the boundary, the date when construction of

Figure 3-1. John Muir School in Long Beach, California, suffered severe damage during the earthquake of March 10, 1933. (Photo courtesy W.L. Huber.)

Figure 3-2. This pre-1933 brick service building at Olive View Hospital in Sylmar, California, collapsed during the 1971 earthquake. (Photo by Mavis Shafer.)

buildings began to include consideration of earthquake forces. Some of the pre-1933 buildings were constructed so loosely that they simply crumbled during earthquakes. Mortar was sometimes of such poor quality that it could barely keep the bricks apart, let alone hold them together. Unreinforced bricks or stones were recognized as being likely to pull apart and collapse with very little ground shaking, so this construction practice was soon abandoned. After 1933, buildings were usually cross-braced and anchored to their foundations, and these techniques improved their earthquake resistance.

The difference in construction practices is the reason that older buildings may be less safe than newer ones. In other respects, some older wood frame buildings may be safer. Before the 1960's, quality homes were built better, in general, than new ones are now. Bigger pieces of lumber were used, and finer craftsmanship resulted in buildings that tended to hold together better during ground shaking.

The idea of earthquake-proof construction is unrealistic, unless exceptionally expensive measures are taken. Any building will collapse if the ground under it shakes hard enough or becomes permanently deformed. But structures can be designed and constructed to incorporate a high degree of earthquake resistance.

Unfortunately, not all modern construction is earthquake resistant. Even if we were to assume that modern building codes ensure that buildings are designed and built with enough flexibility and strength to withstand intense ground shaking, we would also have to believe that planning commissions, landowners, builders, and contractors refrain from building on top of potentially active faults, unstable hillsides, inadequately compacted landfill, reclaimed marshland and tidal flats, and other geologically unsound sites. In addition, we would have to accept on faith that construction materials and practices are of the highest quality, and that tight budgets or deadlines have not forced builders to cut corners. Even if we could depend on a history of consistently high standards of design, site selection, and construction, the fact is that until fairly recently, no one knew very much about the effects of earthquakes on structures.

CITY PLANNING AND LAND USE

Our cities have grown haphazardly. Streets in the older sections followed wagon trails, which had often followed wildlife or Indian trails. Other street plans followed the geography of the area, with the roads following rivers, shorelines, or the base of hills. As settlements expanded, new roads again paralleled or intersected the old, or connected one town with another. Land between the streets was divided and sold again and again.

Buildings were erected, burned or demolished, and built anew. If hurricanes, tornadoes, floods, or earthquakes damaged or destroyed buildings, the land was usually built upon again. Only in the very early settlement days might a location for a town be deemed unsuitable and even abandoned after it was destroyed by a flood, for example. Because of this, owning property in an economically viable area continues to be a strong motivation for developing and using land, regardless of its geologic stability.

Unstable Land.

Faults, landslide areas, or ground subject to liquefaction are identified through earth movement, examination of historic records, or geologic investigation. If the land is privately or publicly owned, there are no laws requiring it to be condemned, zoned for parkland, or bought by the government to keep people from building on it. Except for some California fault zones included in a special program, unstable land can be bought, sold, taxed, and developed just like any other property, unless the owner tries to build something on it that requires special

Figure 3-3. Ground deformation caused the upheaval of this sidewalk and damaged the building. (Photo by Mavis Shafer.)

regulatory zoning, such as a shopping center or high-density housing.

If unstable land is in or close to cities, it has probably been developed, and any earthquake-damaged buildings have most likely been repaired or rebuilt. Before the land in and around cities was smoothed over, paved, sub-divided, terraced, graded, cut, and filled, it may have been possible to recognize landslide areas, crumbling cliffs, floodplains, and earthquake scarps. Now that the obvious features of long-term earth movement have been erased by urban development, we rely on reports from soils engineers and geologists to warn us about unstable building areas. However, this information is rarely volunteered, and is usually only given on new building sites, if those, that are inspected for geologic stability.

In California, the greatest stride toward an effective land use program to reduce earthquake hazards was the passage of the Alquist-Priolo Special Studies Zones Act in 1972. The purpose of the act is to identify active fault zones and prohibit new structures from being built on top of known faults. It requires the State Geologist to delineate areas, called "special studies zones," approximately one-quarter mile wide along traces of active faults. Cities and counties affected by the zones are required to regulate construction projects in which human occupancy structures are planned within the zones according to guidelines established by the California Division of Mines and Geology. Similar zones have been suggested for other states.

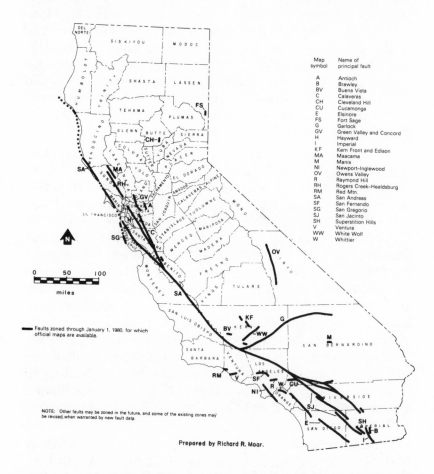

Figure 3-4. Faults in California zoned under the Alquist-Priolo Special Studies Zones Act of 1972. (Map courtesy California Division of Mines and Geology. Prepared by Richard R. Moar.)

Older Structures.

When new ways of construction were devised to improve earthquake resistance, few, if any buildings were rebuilt for that purpose alone, with the exception of schools. Many buildings, which are unsafe due to location, design, or construction, still stand today. Just because an old building has ridden out several earthquakes, doesn't mean that it won't collapse with the next one. But as long as it is economically beneficial, the building will be used—whether or not the unsafe condition is known. It will be expensive to reinforce or rebuild all of these buildings to meet earthquake resistant standards, and the government is unwilling and unable to pay for their reconstruction. Even if a private owner should decide or be required to reinforce an unsafe structure, financing might not be available, ironically, because the building is considered to be high-risk.

Sometimes you can recognize hazardous buildings that date back to the early thirties or earlier. They may be constructed of bricks or very thick concrete, sometimes two or three feet of it. The bricks are separated by crumbling mortar, sometimes set in a distinctive, and weak pattern with every fifth row of bricks laid on end. Often these unsafe structures are hard to distinguish from newer, safer buildings. You might live, work, shop, eat, or worship in one without knowing it. The "cigarette pack" approach has been suggested, labeling these old buildings as hazardous or potentially hazardous. This idea has been rejected, largely because of fear of business losses. In 1980, it was estimated that fifteen to twenty per cent of the population in Los Angeles either lived or worked in an unreinforced masonry building. Other long-established communities would probably have similar if not more disturbing statistics.

Unsafe buildings are of all types: stores, single-family homes, apartment houses, office buildings, warehouses, factories, churches, and restaurants. San Francisco has over ten-thousand earthquake-hazardous buildings. In Los Angeles fifteen years ago, there were eight thousand of them, including two-hundred and twenty one hotels and apartment houses, many of which served low-income and elderly tenants.

The political process to require reinforcing these hazardous old buildings seems to be more complicated than the engineering. In January, 1981, following years

Figure 3-5. Some unreinforced masonry buildings can be recognized by the crumbling mortar or bricks set in a "layer cake" pattern as shown here.

of indecision, the Los Angeles City Council finally enacted controversial safety standards for the city's eight-thousand unreinforced masonry buildings. The familiar arguments were presented: tenants feared rent increases or evictions; demolition would increase the housing crisis; property owners worried about renovation expenses and the limited availability of financing; and structural engineers warned that the buildings could collapse, killing hundreds of people, during an earthquake. The resulting ordinance represented a compromise, a watered-down version of the original proposal, allowing deadlines for full compliance to be extended up to fifteen years, permitting considerable foot-dragging along the way, and requiring that the building meet only about sixty percent of the current earthquake safety standards.

The first to be notified were the private and municipal owners of buildings whose essential services, such as fire, police, telephone, water, and power were essential. Later, notices were sent to the owners of buildings occupied by one-hundred or more people for more than twenty hours a week, then to those with twenty or more occupants, and finally, to those with fewer than twenty occupants. Residential buildings with fewer than five units were not included in the ordinance.

The first phase of the program requires that exterior bearing walls be anchored to the floors and roof. Steel bolts are to be inserted through the exterior walls into the floors and roofs. (See illustration.) Engineers consider this anchoring to be the most important element in improving these old buildings, which pose so great a threat during earthquakes.

Obviously, there are drawbacks to Los Angeles' program. The exemptions and delays allow people to remain—in many cases unknowingly—in buildings so dangerous that a moderate earthquake could cause them to collapse. But welcome progress has been made toward strengthening or eliminating these potential deathtraps. Now nearly complete, the Los Angeles plan has inspired other governmental agencies to begin to address this critical need. In 1986, California enacted a law requiring all cities and counties to identify unreinforced masonry buildings and take steps to mitigate these hazards.

Building Codes.

The standards for construction set by building and safety departments vary among different cities and counties within the United States. Building codes are the "rules" that inspectors enforce as they monitor new construction in progress. When adopted by a city, county, or state, this set of legal documents mandates minimum acceptable standards for factors such as structural design, the number of exits, adequate ventilation, and so forth.

Several building codes are in use in the United States. The Building Officials Conference of America publishes the *Basic Building Code*, used extensively in the Northeast and Midwest. The *Southern Standard Building Code* is most often used in the South, and the *Uniform Building Code* is used mainly on the West Coast, although some cities east of the Rockies have adopted it.

Many major cities have adopted their own codes by modifying one of these model codes. Seismic safety elements are often included in the model codes and are usually omitted from the adopted versions, except in California.

The *Uniform Building Code*, first published in 1927, is the generally accepted standard for building departments in California, and is updated every three years. The Riley Act, adopted by the California Legislature after the 1933 Long Beach earthquake, required almost all buildings to be designed to withstand a lateral force of not less than two percent of the total vertical design load. This means that every building built after 1933 should be able to withstand a lateral force equal to at least two percent of its weight.

Codes set minimum standards considered necessary. However, structures can be much stronger if the builder so chooses, and some engineers design for the strongest

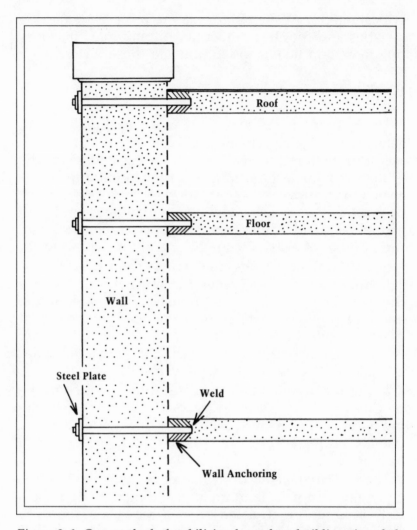

Figure 3-6. One method of stabilizing hazardous buildings is to bolt the walls to floors and roof to prevent the building from pulling apart during an earthquake.

motion anticipated in an earthquake. Buildings designed under the same building code can also differ in earthquake resistance, depending on the architecture and structural materials used.

In general, seismic safety standards are only enacted in areas known to be seismically active within recorded history. This means that the largest earthquake known to have occurred in an area, or the largest one known to have occurred along a fault that passes through an area will be about the largest earthquake anticipated. The relatively short period of recorded history in many areas, and the even shorter period of accurate observation and recording, may prevent a realistic assessment of earthquake risk. Chinese records, which date back three-thousand years, indicate long periods between destructive earthquakes, with some lulls of many hundreds of years. A two-hundred-year history of no destructive quakes in an area may simply be incomplete.

Since 1933, there have been revisions to improve the Riley Act and the *Uniform Building Code*, following recommendations of the Structural Engineers Association of California. Even as the codes change, however, the changes only affect new construction. Many, if not most of the factories, hospitals, homes, power plants, highway bridges, and other facilities in use today were designed with an underestimation of the forces produced by earthquakes, and improvements in the building code are not retroactive.

The 1971 San Fernando earthquake contributed new information about the stresses on building during earthquakes, especially in the field of ground acceleration. This earthquake, which took place on the edge of a metropolitan area of eight million people, was recorded by dozens of specialized strong-motion instruments. It was a moderate earthquake (M6.4), and yet its destruction of new freeways, freeway bridges, and hospitals emphasizes the disparity between the goal and the reality of earthquake resistant construction.

All four hospitals in the immediate area of the San Fernando earthquake were severely damaged. The old 1920s San Fernando Veterans Administration Hospital collapsed, killing forty four people. The newly completed and supposedly earthquake resistant Olive View Hospital was irreparably damaged, causing four deaths. Five dams were fractured, including the Lower Van Norman

Dam, which nearly gave way, threatening the safety of eighty thousand people who had to be evacuated until the reservoir's water could be drained to a safe level. Five freeway overpasses collapsed, and seven more were severely damaged. Many homes, schools, apartments, commercial and industrial buildings, and public structures were also damaged in this "moderate" earthquake.

Certain types of buildings are more vulnerable to earthquake damage. The unreinforced masonry is by far the worst, but other types deserve some mention. Industrial buildings with tilt-up construction (concrete panels tilted up into place to form walls) sometimes pull apart during ground shaking. These buildings need additional work to tie the sides and roof together. Large buildings with a "soft" or open first floor have not performed well in earthquakes. Single family homes usually go through earthquakes very well so long as they are bolted to their foundations. Extra bracing is needed for a garage that supports an upper story.

If buildings built to recent code specifications perform as designed, they should be substantially earthquake resistant—not immune to damage, but unlikely to collapse during severe ground shaking. Engineering and building practices continue to change as more is known about the behavior of structures during earthquake and as structural engineers begin to recognize that the actual forces generated by earthquakes have been vastly underestimated.

The collapse of the double decked Nimitz Freeway in Oakland, California during the 1989 Loma Prieta earthquake was a dramatic reminder that older structures can pose great risks. An ongoing program for strengthening overpasses by the California Department of Transportation (CalTrans), was underway at the time of the earthquake, but budget restraints delayed the process.

Ground acceleration is one measure of the movement of an earthquake. It is measured by strong motion instruments known as accelerographs, which can be installed in buildings or other structures, out in the open, or

Figure 3-7. The new Olive View Hospital had to be demolished after severe damage in 1971 San Fernando earthquake. A massive stairwell unit (at right) separated from the building and fell, as did two similar units. (Photo by Mavis Shafer.)

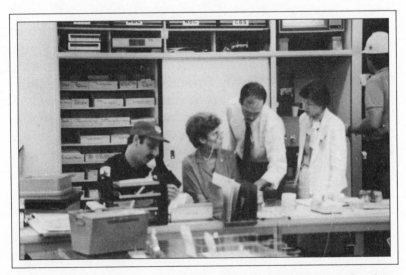

Figure 3-8. Command posts, such as this one at the Los Angeles chapter of the American Red Cross after the Whittier Narrows earthquake, will coordinate disaster response. (Photo courtesy American Red Cross.)

underground. Accelerographs are activated by ground movement and record the amount of force exerted on the place where the instrument is located relative to gravitational pull.

In 1972, the California legislature created the California Strong Motion Instrumentation Program (CSMIP) with the purpose of installing and maintaining strong motion instruments in representative structures and geologic environments throughout California. CSMIP findings are reported to the structural engineering community to be used in the improvement of earthquake resistant design. As a result of this program, the 1979 Imperial Valley, California earthquake was very well instrumented and analysis of those findings has proven to be extremely valuable. For example, in the Imperial County Services Building, which failed (without collapsing, but had to be replaced), data revealed that columns of this open-first story building failed at both the northeast and southwest corners because the building was moving north-south and east-west.

New data was recorded in the 1987 Whittier Narrows, California earthquake in a number of structures, including the California State University, Los Angeles campus, close to the epicenter. The Vincent Thomas suspension bridge, several miles away, provided the first opportunity for study of strong-motion recordings of a bridge. The 1989 Loma Prieta quake provided many accelerograms from strong motion instruments which had been placed in a variety of structures. Unfortunately, they had not been installed on the Bay Bridge or the Nimitz Freeway.

WHO CAN WE DEPEND ON?

We can't depend on government regulations to make sure that all construction is earthquake resistant. We can't even depend on adequate application or enforcement of the regulations we do have. In California, as in most states, each city and county operates its own building department. In small cities and counties, the building department staff may not be qualified to deal with complex engineering problems. Overworked or incompetent building inspectors may overlook problems, which decrease a building's earthquake resistance. In addition, the preparation and use of engineering geology reports may be inadequate or overlooked altogether. Land use decisions may be based on economic and political factors rather than safety. How else can we explain the construction of freeways that follow the fault traces of the Hayward and San Andreas Faults in the San Francisco Bay area, and housing developments that cover sections of those and other known fault zones?

After the Earthquake.

We can't depend on protection after the earthquake either, since the very facilities that are most necessary after a damaging earthquake are often equally vulnerable to earthquake damage, and are not as prepared as we might like to believe. Hospitals, fire departments, transportation, and communication systems may not be available when we need them the most. Even if they are available, they may not be adequate to respond to the scale of the disaster.

One of the biggest problems is communication among levels of government—cities, counties, state, and federal—as well as among the agencies assigned to different jobs—fire, health, police, and civil defense. Delays of precious hours after an earthquake are not inconceivable. Early response to an emergency might be inadequate in any state or country, and this is why individuals need to make their own disaster preparations.

The Seventy-Two Hour Gap.

Most communities have plans to respond to a disaster. Fire departments have agreements to coordinate their response and draw in additional help from unaffected areas. If necessary, the injured will be taken to "casualty collection points" then to be flown to hospitals in other cities or states. Work will begin immediately to open critical highways. The telephone companies have good plans to work on restoring telephone service as quickly as possible. Similar responses are planned for gas, water, and power companies. Temporary morgues will be set up. The American Red Cross will set up shelters and serve meals where there is a need. The Red Cross also assists with damage assessment, personal communication, health services, and individual concerns such as counseling and requesting government assistance.

It will take time to get these programs underway, especially with blocked roads and without telephones. The estimated time is seventy-two hours. It might take less time, or it might take more, depending on the scope of the disaster. Some help will undoubtedly be available earlier than that, but we can't count on it. That's why individuals are urged to plan to be on their own for three days or more. The government can't take care of us, so we have to rely on ourselves.

4

The Earthquake Kit and Other Provisions

If you live in the middle of an open meadow, sheltered by a canvas roof, you can't do much to prepare for an earthquake. Whatever happens out in the open will be beyond your control. A big earthquake out in the country may be frightening to those who are there, but it probably won't be life-threatening unless it triggers landslides, mudflows, or other spectacular geologic events. In cities, though, the structures that people have built, and the places where they have built them, present opportunities for earthquakes to create disaster. And our urban way of life encourages a dependency that often leaves us unprepared to cope with disaster.

Modern cities depend on a system of divided responsibilities, and those who live in an urban environment have learned to rely on the system out of habit. Flip a switch and the lights go on. To get to the twentieth floor, take the elevator. Hungry? Go to a restaurant, fast-food chain, or supermarket. Thirsty? Turn on the water. Need medical assistance? Call the paramedics. Fire? Call the fire department.

An earthquake may cause the system to break down. Call the fire department? How can you call if the telephones don't work? Could you walk or run to the fire station? Do you know where it is? How can fire trucks get to the fire if the roads are blocked with fallen bridges, buildings, and other debris? And what would they use

57

to fight the fire if there's no water pressure? How many fires can they fight at one time? Those of us who depend on the urban system ought to have some idea of how to survive without it. We need to be prepared to take care of ourselves for at least a few days.

Earthquake survival planning is not and cannot be an exact science. There are too many variables. Magnitude, location, and scope of a potential earthquake and the time it will strike are unknown during the planning stage. It would be impossible to be completely prepared for every eventuality. Even attempting to cover every possibility would be so constricting that our everyday lives would have to center on impending disaster—and that would be a disaster in itself.

Once we acknowledge the possibility of damaging earthquakes, however, we can respond with a reasonable number of appropriate measures to reduce the hazards to life and property. To take note of and eliminate the most glaring dangers, and to stock the most necessary provisions—to be aware, in short, of what may happen in an earthquake emergency and to change that which needs changing the most, is the sensible approach.

We recognize that households now consist of single people, single adults with children, adult roommates, couples with children, and various other groupings of ages and relationships. When I mention family or household, I intend it to refer to any person or people living in one apartment, hotel room, condominium, townhouse, duplex, triplex, or house.

THE EARTHQUAKE KIT

First, assemble kits of basic supplies for your home, car, and workplace. The earthquake kit provides the basic equipment and provisions needed to meet most of the initial challenges of a damaging earthquake. Keep one at home, one in each car, and another at work, unless your car is always directly accessible when you are at work.

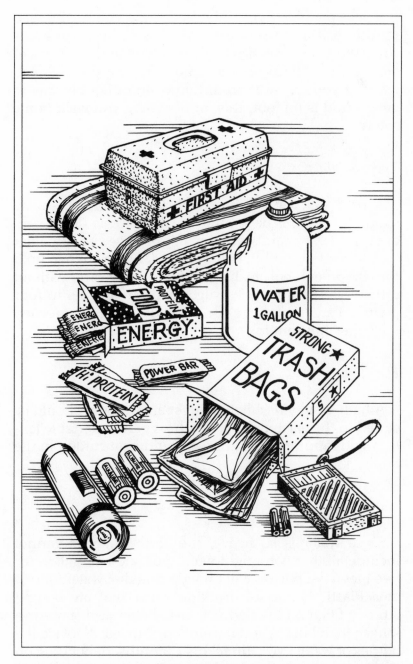

Figure 4-1. The Earthquake Kit. Emergency supplies should be packed in a sturdy container and stored for easy access.

It is impossible to include everything you might need for survival in one compact kit, but these suggestions cover the most basic survival supplies. If you must evacuate, you may have time to grab only one thing as you leave. If you are away from home, and the only way to get around is on foot, this kit may help you walk home safely.

The Container.

A backpack, either the small daypack or the sturdy overnight pack, is best, but a small suitcase, duffle bag, or even a heavy cardboard carton can serve as a container for the earthquake kit. It should be large enough to hold the equipment, but small enough for you to carry without difficulty. The quantities suggested are for one to four people. Larger quantities or extra kits would be needed for larger households.

Flashlight.

A high-quality flashlight with spare batteries should be stored in the earthquake kit. A heavy-duty portable lantern with appropriate batteries could be included in the family kit.

Water.

Since water is so heavy, the earthquake kit cannot include all that you might need, but one-half gallon (or two liters) per person will provide drinking water for one day. Plastic bottles of drinking water that are bought already filled and sealed will taste better and stay fresh longer than bottles you have filled yourself. Replace the bottles of water every three to six months, depending on their exposure to heat and light. Replace the bottles in your car kit every three months.

Food.

Pack one day's supply of high-energy, ready-to-eat food. You don't need to worry about a balanced diet when you

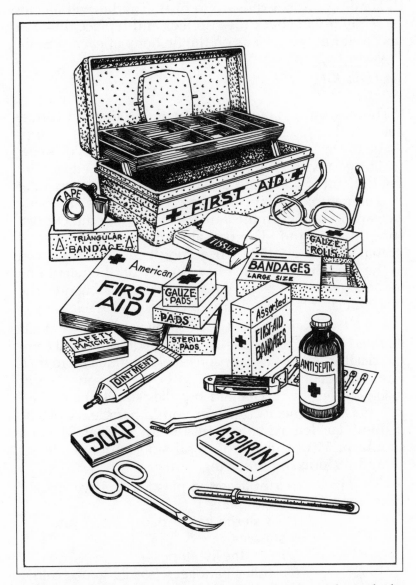

Figure 4-2. The First-Aid Kit. Assemble your own to be ready for earthquakes or other emergencies.

are planning for a quick response to disaster. Pack protein or granola bars, nuts, dried fruit, and other individually packaged lightweight foods such as tuna or fruit in pop-top cans. Replace the food every three to six months, depending on its exposure to heat. The kit will always be ready if you check the supplies and replace the food and water in the car kits on the first day of each season.

First-Aid Kit.

The best preparation for first aid is a first-aid course such as that given by the American Red Cross. Equipment and supplies won't do much good if you don't know what to do with them. Many life-saving procedures are not difficult to learn and don't require any equipment at all. For example, profuse bleeding can be stopped by using a clean cloth or even the bare hand to apply direct pressure on a wound. The first-aid course is good mental preparation in another sense, too. It can accustom you to the idea that you don't have to rely on the telephone for emergencies because, if necessary, you can handle the first crucial moments of an emergency yourself.

A well-stocked first-aid kit complete with a first-aid manual* should be in your earthquake kit. The small commercial first-aid kits usually consist of not much more than a few bandages, so it is best to buy a big one or put together your own. First-aid supplies should be packed in a plastic or metal container with a handle. A plastic (fishing) tackle box with an inside tray is ideal. The box should be clearly marked on all sides. Your home kit should include the following items:

bandages: box of assorted plastic adhesive strips ("bandaids")
12-18 sterile gauze pads (2", 3", and 4" squares)
1 roll adhesive tape
6-8 roller bandages (sterile gauze rolls) 2" & 3"
3 triangle bandages

1 small bar of soap
antibiotic ointment
antiseptic solution
chemical cold compress
small container of table salt
acetaminophen or aspirin tablets
anti-diarrhea medication
scissors
1 card of safety pins, assorted sizes
tweezers for splinter removal
thermometer
tissues
matches
pocket knife (Boy Scout or Swiss Army knife)
three-day supply of medication required or
    frequently used by household members
extra pair of prescription glasses for any household
    members with poor eyesight
sunglasses
contact lens solutions, if needed
first-aid manual*

This household first aid kit, though stored in the earth-quake kit, will help meet any first-aid emergency, whether caused by an earthquake or other sudden need. All liquids should be in plastic containers that are sealed in plastic bags. As medical supplies are used, they should be replaced with new supplies. Medicines are now labeled with expiration dates beyond which their effectiveness might be reduced. Your supplies should be checked annually or more often, and replaced as necessary.

The personal first-aid kits at work and in your car can be smaller, but remember to include eyeglasses and sun-glasses in each. Whenever you renew the prescription and get new glasses, put the old ones in the first-aid kits.

---

*available through the American Red Cross and book stores

Portable Radio and Batteries.

You can probably use your car radio, provided that you can get to your car and car keys following an earthquake. But a portable radio stored in your earthquake kit would be more convenient. Store a sufficient number of alkaline batteries of the right size outside the radio in a small plastic bag or in their original packages. It is important that the batteries be alkaline; the storage life of alkaline batteries is over a year under normal conditions (even longer if refrigerated) and they will not leak as carbon-zinc batteries can.

Keeping the batteries outside the radio ensures that their power will not be drained in the event that the radio is accidentally turned on or if there happens to be a slight electrical short in the radio itself. This also prevents old, leaking batteries from damaging the radio.

Some sporting goods stores sell a wind-up radio, which eliminates the concern about dead batteries. After a disaster, radio stations will broadcast emergency instructions, as well as other facts as they become available.

Walking Shoes and Socks.

Comfortable, thick-soled walking shoes should be included in your kits in the car and at work. If the roads are blocked, the only transportation may be on foot. Be sure that your shoes are suitable for long distances and for walking over piles of broken glass.

Jacket, Hat, Comfortable Clothes.

That long walk home will be easier if you have jeans, a sweatshirt, jacket, and hat to keep you warm and comfortable. In hot weather, a hat will help keep you cool and shade your eyes. These won't be necessary in your home kit, because you'll probably have access to your clothing at home.

Plastic Trash Bags.

Include four to eight large heavy-duty trash bags. They don't take up much room or add much weight to the kit, and you might not even need them; however, they could be essential in keeping you dry or providing temporary shelter. Keeping dry is very important, especially if the weather is cold or if you have been injured.

The scissors, tape, and pins in the first-aid kit could help you transform the trash bags into rain gear, wind protection, shade, or other shelter. For quick protection from rain and wind, tear a small slit (about six inches) on the side of the bag near the bottom. Put the bag over your head, pushing your face through the opening slit. It will look pretty silly, but it works. Tall people can use a second bag by ripping out the bottom, stepping into the bag, and securing it around the waist.

Local Map and Directions to Community Services.

If people in your household are not familiar with walking routes around the local community, a street map should be included in the earthquake kit. Be sure that you know the best walking route between your home and work and, if applicable, to your child's school.

A Blanket.

Any injury can cause shock, but the fright of an earthquake experience might make a shock reaction even more likely. Blankets help prevent the loss of body heat, a factor that must be considered when treating shock victims.

To save space in your car and work kits, buy an emergency or "space" blanket for each person. These are very lightweight, full-sized sheets which fold into a 4" x 2" x 2" space. They keep you warm by retaining your body heat.

Sanitation Supplies.

Include small and medium zip-lock plastic bags for human waste disposal, small packages of tissues, pre-moistened towelettes, and sanitary napkins.

Heavy-Duty Work Gloves.

For lifting or climbing through debris, gloves will protect your hands.

Communication Kit.

Use a small zip-lock plastic bag to hold a few stamped postcards addressed to your out of town contact and others you might want to write to if telephone service is out for several days. Keep a couple of pens to write with, a list of important phone numbers, and a few dollars in change to use at a pay phone. You wouldn't try to use the phone right after the earthquake unless you had a life-threatening emergency, but several hours later, pay phones might be working, even when the regular ones are not.

Sleeping Bag.

If you have to spend a few days at work, a sleeping bag will help make you more comfortable. This is optional equipment, depending on your personal situation.

OTHER PROVISIONS

In addition to the provisions stored in your earthquake kits, the following items should be available in your home and at work to be ready for an earthquake:

Fire Extinguishers.

Many experts recommend the powdered sodium bicarbonate fire extinguisher for kitchens, because it is very effective on Class B (burning grease), and suitable for

Class C (electrical fires) as well. The ABC dry chemical extinguisher is effective in the kitchen, too. An extinguisher with a hose and nozzle attached is recommended. In the garage, office, or any other area, use an ABC multipurpose extinguisher such as 2A;40BC or the larger 4A;60BC UL rating. Your local fire department may recommend the number and size extinguishers needed for your home.

The halon fire extinguisher puts out a fire by its nonconductive halon gas smothering the fire. To be effective, it must be used in an enclosed room. The major advantage to the halon extinguisher is that it leaves no residue like the dry-chemical models. For this reason, halon is selected for protecting electronic gear such as computers. The main drawbacks to halon gas are environmental; the halon gas may damage the earth's ozone layer. If you choose to buy a halon extinguisher, be sure to look for the UL rating and pick the appropriate size and type for your needs.

The gauge at the top of the extinguisher indicates whether the unit has sufficient pressure to operate. Check it monthly at home and, if it is your responsibility, at work, to be sure that there hasn't been a pressure loss, which would keep the unit from working. If the extinguisher has been used, it must be recharged. To recharge, check the Yellow Pages for a fire extinguisher servicing company. Each extinguisher should be securely mounted to the studs of the wall and located where it will be readily visible when needed. Be sure that all household members or co-workers know its location and how to operate it.

Extra Flashlights.

At least one working flashlight per person should be kept in the home and workplace. Keep one at each bedside. Each should be kept in a location known to all, and in such a way that an earthquake won't be likely to make it inaccessible. You might hang it on a hook or tuck it in a drawer. If you keep a flashlight on top of a bedside table or on an open shelf, it could slide off during an earth-quake and be difficult to find. It's also important to be consistent about where flashlights are kept so that you can find one easily in the dark.

To simplify battery replacement, most or all of the disposable-battery flashlights in the home should use the same size battery. Be sure to keep extra bulbs and batteries on hand. Alkaline batteries last longer than the standard "heavy duty" batteries, and extras will last longer if they're kept refrigerated.

Rechargeable flashlights and lanterns have added a new dimension to disaster planning. On the one hand, the lights that stay plugged into an electrical outlet or charging stand are always fully charged when the power goes off, so you won't have to worry about finding your flashlight with the batteries dead. On the other hand, if the power is going to stay off, there won't be any way to recharge the light once its charge is drained, and the light only lasts from one to three hours.

Another type of rechargeable battery is the type that is not plugged in until the battery is very low, and then is recharged by plugging in the recharger for a limited number of hours. The drawback to this type is that it may not be fully charged at the time the power goes off. There are solar rechargers available for NiCad batteries, and these would be very useful in a long-term blackout. I think that a combination of power sources would be best for flashlights at home.

Open flames, such as in candles, matches, and cigarette lighters, would not be wise to use as light sources fol-lowing an earthquake because of the danger of gas leaks and other fire hazards. Aftershocks can also cause candle holders and kerosene lanterns to topple over, increasing the risk of fire and burns.

Some alternative light sources are not fire hazards. Liquid fuel emergency candles self-extinguish when they are tipped over. Some of these provide light for up to fifty hours. Light sticks, plastic sticks filled with two chemi-cals that are mixed by flexing the stick, give off a glow of light when activated. Although they aren't very bright, they do last about eight hours, have a long shelf life, and are relatively inexpensive to store in several locations. The light sticks would be especially appropriate for children, because they are non-toxic and unbreakable. They are available in hardware, sporting goods stores, and even some grocery stores.

Power Failure Lights.

These flashlights are kept plugged into electrical outlets and turn on automatically when the power goes off. Depending on the size of your home, keep one or more plugged into outlets in the hallway, stairway, or bedroom to help in evacuating safely. They can be removed from the outlet and used as a flashlight, but remember that most power failure lights only provide about an hour's light after the power goes off. Their chief value is in lighting up the darkened room as soon as the power is off.

Tools for Turning Off Utilities.

All adults in the household should know the location of all the main turn-off valves for the home and how to use them. Gas and water lines inside the house usually have valves near their outlets. For example, there are shut-off valves under sinks and toilets, and gas lines can be shut off near their connections to gas appliances. For gas, the general rule is that if the handle is parallel to the gas pipe, the valve is open; if perpendicular to the pipe, it is closed. (See illustration.) It might be faster, and therefore safer, to first turn off the gas or water near the damaged line, if it is easily accessible, and then go outside to turn off the main line.

Most natural gas main valves are located outside the house or building, near the meter, and are operated with a crescent wrench or specially designed tool. The shut-off valve is on the pipe that takes gas from the main to the meter. Use a wrench to give the valve a one-quarter turn in either direction so that it will be cross-wise to the pipe. (See illustration.) Some water mains also require a special tool. Store the appropriate tools near the valves.

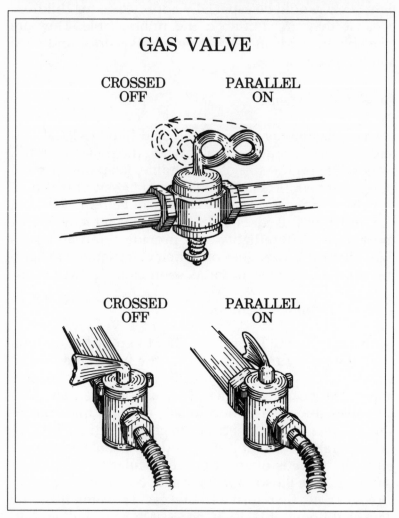

Figure 4-3. To turn off the gas inside a building, turn the valve so that it will go across the gas line, as shown.

Other Tools.

Rescue work, setting up evacuation areas, and debris removal will be much easier with the proper tools. Many

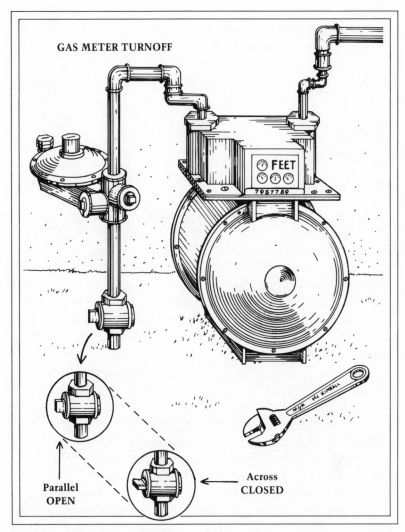

GAS METER TURNOFF

Parallel
OPEN

Across
CLOSED

Figure 4-4. Use a wrench to give the valve a one-quarter turn in either direction to shut off the gas.

of these items would already be on hand at home and in many businesses.

Crowbar
Work gloves (already included in earthquake kits)
hard hats
shovel

knife
screw driver
hammer
duct tape
axe
broom
dustpan
tarpaulin
pen, paper, adhesive labels

Additional Water.

Drinking water is more important than food for a short-term emergency, so plan to have a supply of water beyond that which is in your earthquake kits. Aside from the liquids stored in the refrigerator and melted ice cubes, canned goods are another source of liquid. Drinking water will also be available in the water heater and toilet tank (unless chemical cleaners are used in the tank). Be sure that the water heater is secured as described in Chapter 5 to protect it.

Store one gallon of water per person per day—double in desert climates—stored in sealed plastic containers in a cool, dark place. This includes water for sanitation as well as drinking. Five-gallon plastic bottles of drinking water can be purchased from drinking water suppliers; one-gallon and two-liter bottles are generally available in supermarkets. The five-gallon bottles, if kept sealed and stored in a cool, dark place, will stay drinkable indefinitely. Smaller bottles have a shelf life of about six months to a year, depending on temperature and smog. Small bottles are easier to handle, an important consideration for people who would have difficulty pouring from a five-gallon bottle. Manufacturers of disaster supplies sell emergency drinking water packed in cans, boxes, or heavy foil packets.

If you have extra freezer space, fill clean, empty milk cartons with water and store them in the freezer. The blocks of ice will keep your freezer cold longer when the power is off, and the melted ice will be fine for drinking.

Extra Food.

It's a good idea to store at least three days' supply of food in addition to the day's supply in the earthquake kit. After a disaster, it may be some time before stores can be restocked. They may open to sell existing inventory after a few days, but it may be a long time before "business as usual." That's why some people recommend keeping a two week or longer supply of everything you might need.

If the electricity is off, perishables in the refrigerator will not last long; frozen foods will thaw gradually, if the freezer is kept closed. Besides perishable goods, you will probably have some canned or packaged foods on hand. In workplaces that might become isolated following an earthquake—such as a high-rise building—three days' supply of food and water should be stored.

Food supplies could consist of specially purchased disaster rations, camping food such as freeze-dried packages, or an assortment of ready-to-eat packaged and canned food with a manual can opener or pop-top cans. Camping stores and many sporting goods stores sell easy-to-prepare, lightweight, freeze-dried foods. These foods keep for extended periods of time, but they do require lots of water, usually hot, to prepare. If you choose to store the freeze-dried foods, be sure to store additional water and a way of heating water.

Disaster rations can be purchased from vendors who specialize in emergency supplies. These foods have a long shelf life, usually five years. They can be "energy" bars or individual meals sealed in "retort" bags. They do not require heating or additional water. This disaster food is ideal for businesses and for anyone who would like to store disaster food in the easiest way possible.

Be sure that you and the other household members like the taste of the food that you store. An earthquake is upsetting enough without having to eat food that you don't like. I usually keep things on hand that I consider "comfort foods," like chicken soup with an extra can of chicken to add to it, and the family's favorite granola bars.

If you are storing standard canned and packaged foods, you can either keep a large supply on hand at all times or keep the disaster supply in a place separate from the regular pantry. If you store it separately, plan to replace it annually. If you keep all stored food together, be sure to rotate it. When you buy fresh supplies, put the new cans and packages in the back of the cupboard and move the older ones forward. To be sure that your supplies are fresh, look for the manufacturer's expiration date. If there is none, use a grease pencil to label the cans and packages with the date as you put them away. Once a year, clean out the cupboard; if anything is a year old, use it up or throw it away. Manufacturers generally recommend that canned goods have a shelf-life of one year; after that, the food might begin to deteriorate.

A selection of foods from the basic food groups should be your goal, but remember special food needs such as baby food and pet food. Napkins, pre-moistened towelettes, a manual can opener, paper or plastic plates, cups, and bowls, and eating utensils should be stored with the food. Don't store salty foods because they increase thirst.

Some suggestions of foods that do not require heating include:

> dry-roasted, unsalted peanuts or almonds
> trail mix
> peanut or almond butter
> high protein bars, "breakfast bars," diet meal bars
> granola bars
> canned tuna (water-packed), salmon, chicken, or
>   turkey
> canned or boxed fruit juices
> canned fruit or applesauce
> raisins and other dried fruits, dried fruit rolls
> crackers or cold cereals (in airtight containers)
> instant drink mix
> packaged, canned, or powdered milk
> canned brown bread
> canned sandwich spread

hard candy
honey

All of these foods can be eaten at room temperature with no preparation or cooking. Since you probably won't be able to refrigerate leftovers, store only single-portion or single meal-sized cans.

It is not difficult to plan for some limited heating of food as part of your disaster planning. If you have a camp stove, be sure that you always have some extra fuel on hand. Canned liquid fuel (Sterno®) stoves or chafing dishes can also be used, as can your barbecue, which would require extra charcoal and lighter fluid on hand.

Remember when using any of these heating methods after an earthquake that aftershocks are expected. Do your cooking outside on a fire-proof surface, preferably on the ground, to limit possible danger from spills. Remember to store any hazardous fuels very safely, and keep matches on hand. If you are planning to heat foods away from home, remember to include a pan and utensils for cooking. If you plan to heat water or food, some easy-to-prepare foods include:

tea bags*, instant coffee, hot chocolate mix*
bouillon or instant soup*
canned soups
canned chili, hash, beef stew, spaghetti, baked beans
hot cereal*

Sanitation Supplies.

When the water is turned off, sanitation becomes a problem. Storing supplies in advance will help considerably when the time comes. If there has been damage to sewer lines, the toilets won't flush. They won't flush if there isn't any water, either. The easiest solution to this problem is to line the toilet with a plastic bag, or if no toilet is available (in your evacuation area, for example),

---

sealed for storage in plastic bags

use a sturdy bucket or waste basket lined with a plastic bag. After use, remove the plastic bag, seal it, and place it in a trash can away from people. A camper's portable toilet can also be used.

In the discussion on water storage, water for sanitation has been included with the drinking water. Swimming pool water can also be used for flushing toilets (if the sewer lines are intact) or for washing.

In addition to water, these supplies are recommended:

kitchen-sized plastic trash bags (toilet liners), twist ties
bucket, small trash can, or other container for
    portable toilet (or camp toilet)
toilet paper
paper towels
household bleach
disinfectant
matches
soap
liquid detergent
large plastic trash bags for trash disposal
sanitary napkins (also work well for first-aid dressings)
toothbrush, toothpaste, shampoo, deodorant, comb,
    and other personal hygiene supplies

Storage.

As you're beginning to stock all these supplies, you may wonder where to store them. There are several alternatives. For some items, it's easy. One fire extinguisher goes in the kitchen, because that's where most fires start. If you have a large home, keep another extinguisher upstairs or at the other end of the house, and one in the garage.

There should be a working flashlight at each bedside, with shoes or slippers with thick soles, work gloves, and a bathrobe or clothes you can jump into quickly. If you wear glasses, keep them at the bedside, too.

The earthquake kits go in the car and, if necessary, at work. The home earthquake kit should be in a closet near an exit. The family first-aid kit should be at the top of the kit for easy access in non-earthquake emergencies.

Some people keep the rest of their supplies in a "disaster closet or cupboard." Others use a new, large plastic trash can with a tight fitting lid. They fill it with supplies, seal it with tape, and store it on a patio, apartment balcony, or in the garage. Others keep their disaster supplies in with their other supplies. Wherever you store them, remember to check all supplies at least once a year, and replace what is missing, past its expiration date, or too old.

Automatic Gas Shut-Off Valves.

The most controversial of all earthquake-protection devices are the automatic gas shut-offs. These devices are installed on the gas line between the meter and the building served. When the device is shaken, the valve closes. After the valve is closed, the gas must be turned on by a licensed plumber or gas service person. The devices are usually adjusted to shut off the gas in the event of shaking equivalent to a potentially damaging earthquake. The manufacturers claim that minor shaking, such as that of a big truck going by, won't activate the shut-off valves.

On one side of the controversy are the gas and utility companies, who oppose the devices. Their opposition is primarily due to the increased workload that would be created after an earthquake if many people installed the shut-off valves. A gas serviceperson must turn on all the gas turned off by the automatic valves. Many, if not most of the valves, would have been activated unnecessarily; that is, there would not have been a gas leak caused by the earthquake, but the gas would have been turned off. The gas companies also criticize the valves for being too sensitive to minor shaking and too likely to shut off the gas when it would not be necessary.

In general, fire departments like the shut-off valves. It is true that leaking gas is one of the most common causes of fires following earthquakes, and the shut-off valves will reduce that risk. Fire department spokespersons also point out that many gas valves are "frozen" shut or stuck, and that when people try to turn off the valves in an emergency, they sometimes can't turn the valve.

Clearly, automatic shut-off valves are a good idea for many people, especially for those who have an impaired sense of smell or who would be unable to turn off the gas themselves, and for mobile homes, which shake easily. There are more important pieces of safety equipment, such as fire extinguishers, so automatic shut-offs would not be a top priority, but overall, I think they are a good idea for many people.

EARTHQUAKE INSURANCE

Homeowner's insurance and fire insurance policies don't cover damage caused by earthquakes unless you have paid for a rider or attachment to your policy for this additional coverage. The policy to cover earthquake damage is usually attached to a fire insurance policy covering fire damage to your house, condominium, or apartment, or to the homeowner's or renter's policy, which covers several types of damage or loss. The amount covered by the earthquake rider must be the same as the amount covered by the main policy. The earthquake rider usually covers volcanic eruption damage as well. If you live along the coast, you should make sure that your policy includes tsunami coverage.

If you already have fire insurance or homeowner's insurance, you can add earthquake coverage in most cases by calling your insurance agent and asking for it. You don't have to wait until the expiration date of your policy. Don't wait until there's a major earthquake, though, because most companies won't write new policies during the few weeks after a major earthquake because of the danger of aftershocks.

The earthquake rider is fairly expensive, now about two dollars per thousand dollars of coverage, usually with a ten percent deductible. This means that if the house is insured for $100,000, the first $10,000 in damage will not be covered. Masonry veneer (bricks or rocks covering the outside of a building) is usually not covered unless you pay a higher premium. Check with your insurance agent about replacement value coverage when you discuss earthquake insurance. This rider applies to the main policy, but it usually includes the earthquake coverage. With replacement value coverage, personal property would be covered for the amount needed to replace a destroyed item rather than what the used item was worth. With earthquake damage, replacement value coverage would certainly reduce the out-of-pocket expenses following the earthquake.

The vast majority of people don't buy earthquake insurance. Following a local earthquake, insurance agents typically receive many calls from people wanting to add earthquake coverage. But after a year or so passes without a significant tremor, many cancel the coverage to save money, saying, "What the heck ... I'll take a chance."

Earthquake insurance is the same kind of gamble as life insurance. The only way you win is by losing. But if a moderate or larger earthquake strikes nearby, earthquake insurance could mean protection from financial ruin. I think that it's worth the expense for some people. With continually rising housing costs, many people have committed themselves to large and costly mortgages. Others have their life savings tied up in the equity of their home. Inflated building costs might make the expense of repairing earthquake damage staggering.

If you own your own home or condominium in any seismically active region, there is always the possibility, however remote, that an earthquake could destroy it and leave you with mortgage payments still due. On the other hand, if the earthquake risk in your area is low, and your home is unlikely to be severely damaged by an earthquake, the special coverage may not be a good investment. Whether or not you purchase earthquake coverage, the best earthquake insurance is to reduce the structural and non-structural hazards in the building.

Some people don't carry earthquake coverage because they believe that if a disastrous earthquake strikes, the area would probably be declared a federal disaster area, making them eligible for federal disaster benefits. These people may not realize that disaster relief is almost always in the form of low-interest loans. If they already owe money on their property, as most people do, they will be required to pay off the original loans as well as the new disaster loan. If some portion of the disaster loan is "waived," or not required to be repaid, it probably won't be much. In addition, federal assistance may be delayed for months and may not be sufficient to compensate for the extent of the damage and for housing until the repairs have been completed.

Repairing the home to its pre-earthquake condition will not add to its previous value. In fact, equity in the home may be significantly reduced or even lost, and some people may find themselves indebted for more than the value of their home. To further aggravate the situation, the housing market in the stricken area usually drops in the aftermath of an earthquake, only to remain depressed for several months or longer. Some owners may be forced to sell at a loss.

There is some question as to whether insurance companies could fulfill claims even for the relatively small amount of earthquake coverage they now issue in the event of a great earthquake. Federal backing may be needed to underwrite a realistic earthquake insurance program. National earthquake insurance, compulsory coverage for all natural disasters, and local insurance through property taxes are some of the solutions proposed.

5

Preparing the Home and Workplace

MAKING PLANS

Talk about your earthquake plans with household members and co-workers. They may not react with logic and cooperation. You may even have trouble getting them to talk about it. Some people don't like to talk about emergency plans because of a superstition that somehow talking about a disaster will cause it to happen. Other people don't want to talk about dangerous situations because they don't trust themselves. They are afraid that they won't react appropriately in an emergency, or won't be brave. These concerns are normal; after all, we don't know what dangers will face us or how we will react to them, but talking about it may help dispel some of the anxiety. At least, when the earthquake does happen, it won't be the first time that we've considered what to do.

Cooperative Planning.

Teenagers and adult members of the household should share in the preparations for an earthquake. Getting your home ready, selecting safe refuges, and making contingency plans should be shared. Be sure that all immunizations are up to date. If you have special needs, such as a disabled person in the household, or a particular hazard near your home, you will need to make special

81

preparations. Locate the emergency facilities (fire, police, and hospital) closest to your home and work. Many families have drills to practice what to do during and after an earthquake.

Reunification Plans.

Families should decide together where to meet in the event of a disaster striking when they are separated. Will the family members who are at work or college go home? Will they meet somewhere else? Who will pick the children up at school? Remember that there may be no way to travel except on foot following a damaging earthquake, and that telephones should not be used after any earthquake except to report a serious emergency, so the plan must be simple and consistent.

It may take days for some people to get home. School personnel are obligated, both morally and legally, to stay on the job during a disaster for up to seventy-two hours or until they are released by their supervisors. People who work in high-rise buildings or long distances from home may be unable to get home for two or three days. The reunion plan must consider these possibilities.

The anxiety of being separated from the ones you love may be something you will have to deal with for a few hours or even days, but it will be easier to handle if you have considered the possibility beforehand. It would undoubtedly be easier to face a disaster with your loved ones, but just because you happen not to be together is no reason to assume that the other person is dead or injured. Try to have every member of your family prepared to deal appropriately with any emergency, and then trust their good sense and knowledge to help them through.

Safe Refuge.

Identify an evacuation area near your home where the family can get together after a damaging earthquake to wait for aftershocks, evaluate the situation, and make plans for appropriate action. It should be a place in the open, away from anything that can fall on you. It could be your backyard, front yard, driveway, a parking lot, nearby park, or even the sidewalk. After the ground stops shaking, and after you've taken care of injuries, fires and fire hazards, and building inspection, you might decide to carefully evacuate to the safe refuge.

Many people feel more comfortable outdoors after an earthquake, because it is usually the safest place to be during an earthquake. Following a damaging quake, aftershocks are definitely expected, and there is always the possibility that the earthquake you've just felt is a foreshock for a larger one. If you have patio furniture, or sleeping bags spread out on a tarpaulin, you can rest comfortably in your evacuation area (after all needed inspections are complete) and listen to the portable radio for information. If you feel more comfortable remaining indoors after determining that it is safe, it is not necessary to evacuate.

There are some places, especially downtown in big cities, where it is safer to remain inside after an earthquake, so long as there are no fires, chemical spills, or structural damage in the building. In some downtown areas, there are no open places far enough from glass and other debris which might be falling. When windows in high-rise buildings break, the glass doesn't always fall straight down. As the building sways, the glass can be catapulted or catch a wind current and glide great distances. The sidewalks, streets, parking lots, and lawns below tall buildings are not safe places to be during or after an earthquake because of the danger of falling objects. Aftershocks can cause additional damage, causing more glass to break and fall.

At work, the evacuation area is usually determined by the disaster coordinator, who would also decide when it is necessary to evacuate after an earthquake. Sometimes, in areas with tall buildings where debris might be falling, the evacuation area is indoors, for example, in an underground parking garage.

Out-of-Town Contact.

One out-of-town relative or friend should be asked to assist large or extended families, which may include several households in different locations within a city. Following an emergency, it is possible that long distance telephone service will be restored before local service. In this case, family members can use the out of town contact to relay messages or set up meetings. If there is a long delay in restoring telephone service, send a post card or letter to your contact person, and to any others you need to reach. Even after an earthquake, the mail will go through, although it may be delayed.

EVALUATING THE BUILDING

When we select a home, most of us don't consider evaluating its earthquake vulnerability, but we should. There are certain locations and types of buildings that should be avoided altogether. And there are others in which improvements can be made to upgrade earthquake safety. People who rent or lease their homes may not be able or willing to undertake any structural modifications, but the arrangement of interior furnishings can do much to reduce hazards. Information about a particular building's dangers may help you avoid injury during and after an earthquake. If, for example, you know that one exit may be dangerous after an earthquake, you can use another.

Before investing, it is always wise to have the building professionally inspected by a company licensed for that purpose. The inspector will evaluate the earthquake safety of the building by looking at its location and structural characteristics, and make recommendations for any necessary improvements. If you are renting or leasing your home, follow the guidelines in this chapter for evaluating the building. Then, reduce the hazards in each room.

Location.

Obvious areas to avoid or be very careful about include fault zones, unstable soils, which might experience liquefaction or uneven settling, slide-prone hillsides, and spillways of dams, reservoirs, and storage tanks. Consult a geologist or soils engineer for a thorough evaluation of the geology, or take a look at a geologic map of the area. These maps are often available at the local library, by request from the U.S. Geological Survey or the state division of mines and geology. In California, when property is sold within the Alquist Priolo Special Studies Zones (the major fault zones), the buyers must be informed so that they may better evaluate the decision.

Whenever you select a home, you should take a good look at the surrounding area in as many ways as possible. Look around for significant cracks in the earth, streets, retaining walls, and driveways. Be aware of the type of industrial facilities, if any, nearby, as well as railroad tracks, freeways, and highways.

Figure 5-1. The moderate (M6.2) earthquake in Morgan Hill, California, on April 24, 1984, caused this contemporary home to slide off the foundation. (Photo courtesy Bill Gates.)

Figure 5-2. This home suffered severe damage, partly because the garage did not provide a stable foundation for the second story. (Photo courtesy Los Angeles Department of Building and Safety.)

Structural Characteristics.

For earthquake resistance, unreinforced masonry is the most hazardous type of construction, and single story wood frame is the best. Other structural elements to consider are, first, that the frame of the building is connected to the foundation; secondly, that design does not operate against earthquake safety. Large expanses of glass may weaken the structure, and complicated architecture involving many exterior corners and wings may reduce the building's ability to flex as a unit. Lateral bracing or shear walls are now recommended. Garages that serve as foundations for rooms above them may need additional bracing for earthquake resistance. Heavy roofing material, such as clay tile, may weaken the structure, and may fall off during ground shaking. Slender stilts for vertical support may not perform well under stress. Chimneys installed before 1960 may not be properly reinforced and tied to the building. Be especially careful about very tall chimneys, which could fall in the direction of an exit.

Pre-1935 buildings may have special problems relating to poor design or maintenance, or improper repair of previous earthquake damage. A structural engineer can evaluate and advise about correcting these concerns.

PREPARING EVERY ROOM

It isn't practical or even possible to earthquake-proof everything. No matter how well you tie things down, there may still be damage, depending on the size of the earthquake, and you can go through small earthquakes with no preparation and no damage. We try to surround ourselves with things that can be used or enjoyed every day, and they can't all be tied down or permanently anchored. But glaring hazards can and should be eliminated, and we should try to protect things that have great value to us or to the world.

The Kitchen.

When the 1971 earthquake shook our house in Sylmar, most of the cupboard doors in the kitchen, bathrooms,

Figure 5-3. The chimney of this suburban home collapsed during the 1971 San Fernando earthquake and crashed through the patio roof. (Photo courtesy Los Angeles Department of Building and Safety.)

Figure 5-4. This unreinforced masonry chimney collapsed during the 1971 San Fernando earthquake, destroying the porch of this older home. (Photo courtesy Los Angeles Department of Buildings and Safety.)

garage, and laundry room opened, throwing their contents onto the floor. Almost everything on open shelves slid off. The refrigerator leaned forward and opened to empty its stock. Syrup, milk, oil, grape juice, flour, vinegar, sugar, and five gallons of drinking water oozed around cereal boxes, spice jars, and the remains of our dishes, glassware, crystal, and just about everything else that hadn't been nailed down. The odors produced by this conglomeration vied for attention with the perfume/after shave/shampoo deposits in the bathroom sinks and floor. It took us hours to find our car keys.

One stroke of luck was that the dishwasher was full of clean dishes, loaded on racks to protect against the pulsing water and, unexpectedly, earthquake shaking, so nothing inside it was broken. Much later, as I compiled a list of losses for our tax return, I realized that one cupboard hadn't opened, and nothing inside it was broken. The latch on that cupboard had always been stiff.

Besides the mess to clean up, and the breakage, there is danger to anyone who happens to be in an unprepared kitchen during an earthquake. Shattering glass, spattering chemicals, fire, and falling objects (light fixtures, hanging utensils, and objects sliding off counters, shelves, and cupboards) can injure anyone in the way.

Figure 5-5. Strong cupboard latches would prevent this kind of damage during an earthquake. (Photo by Mavis Shafer.)

With the goal of preventing injury and reducing damage, these suggestions can be used to begin your earthquake precautions, according to your own needs and priorities.

- Install earthquake latches on cupboard doors. Catches designed for use in campers are ideal, because they will not open if the cupboard is tilted or shaken. Heavy objects inside your cupboards can lean or fall against the inside of the cabinet doors, and the latches must be strong enough to withstand this pushing. The "passive" latches, which automatically lock when the door is closed, would be best for families with people who might forget to latch the door. The "child-proof" guards for cupboard doors can also serve as earthquake guards, and these are not visible from the outside. The relatively simple and inexpensive precaution of installing earthquake catches can save you hundreds of dollars, while preventing serious injuries.

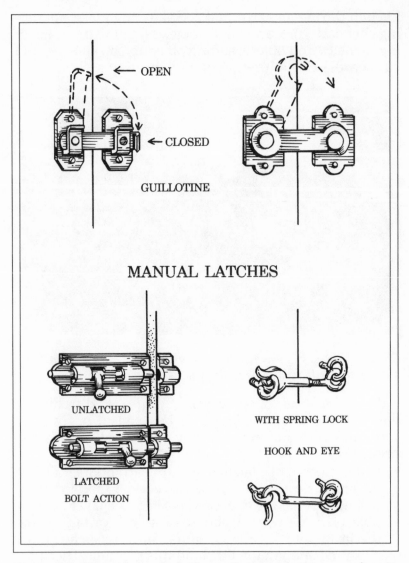

OPEN

CLOSED

GUILLOTINE

MANUAL LATCHES

UNLATCHED

WITH SPRING LOCK

HOOK AND EYE

LATCHED
BOLT ACTION

Figure 5-6. Remember to lock the cupboard each time you close it.

- Store heaviest items on lower shelves of lower cabinets. Heavy things may break through a cupboard door, but they probably won't hurt anyone if they are at floor level. Don't store heavy and light objects together. Heavy things can tip or slide over and crush lighter objects.

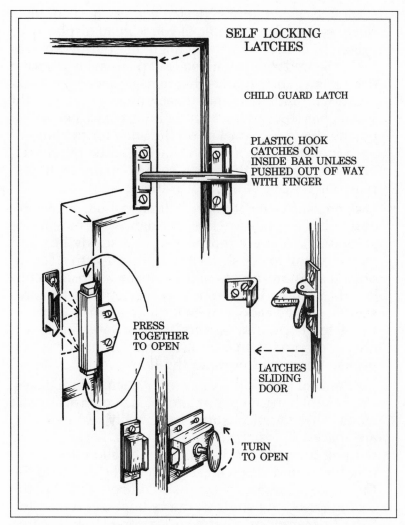

Figure 5-7. These latches lock automatically each time you close the cupboard.

- Put guard rails or "fences" on open shelves so that items can't slide off. If you want to display fragile things on open shelves, silicon adhesive, or pressure-sensitive, industrial strength Velcro® tape, called "Quake Tape®," or the related Quake Grip® products can be used. Florists clay is no longer recommended because it deteriorates with age.

For special situations, devise your own earthquake safety system. For example, if you want to display your collection of beer mugs, you might use narrow shelves with a lip and a guardrail made of piano wire or strong fishing line, and separate the mugs by a wooden backboard with indentations for each mug. Or you might install pegs over which each mug could be placed upside down, or "tracks" on the shelf for the base of each mug to slide between. Racks can be purchased or made, and after the rack is secured to the shelf, display objects can be placed in the rack.

- Pack breakables for storage. Delicate crystal, stemware, and china are safest when packed as for moving or shipping: wrapped and packed in a sturdy box and stored on the lower shelf of a cupboard with a secure door. For more accessibility, use racks inside cupboards, anchored to the shelf. Some department stores sell soft quilted caddies with individual compartments for plates, cups, and saucers, or stemware. These will offer good protection so long as you prevent the whole package from sliding onto the floor.

- Secure wall and ceiling fixtures. Attach light fixtures, clocks, and hanging plants and kitchen utensils to wall studs. These vertical supports, usually two-by-fours, are spaced 16" apart, inside the walls. Locate one by tapping the wall and listening for a solid rather than a hollow sound. Then measure along the wall to locate the others. Hanging fixtures should be secured to the ceiling joists (the studs in the ceiling) or even better, to a two-by-four or other board fastened to the ceiling joists. Fixtures screwed into plaster, wallboard, or paneling, are more likely to fall, and could take some of the wall or ceiling with them.

- Safely store household chemicals, especially those that are flammable or caustic, so that they will neither fall nor spill. Storage at floor level in secured cabinets is best. There are plastic caddies for cleaning supplies, which can be used for storing products so that they won't tip over. Dishwasher detergent, drain cleaners,

Figure 5-8. Household goods should be stored with heavy items on lower shelves and lightweight ones above.

oven cleaners, lighter fluid, and ammonia are some of the most dangerous chemicals. Periodically discard dangerous products you don't often use. When buying such products, it's best to buy just enough for one particular job rather than buying a five-year supply of

something you only use once or twice a year. Don't
buy dangerous products in glass containers.
- Install stoves and other gas appliances with flexible gas
  lines.
- Store extra keys on cup hooks so that you can find
  them in a hurry.
- Block heavy appliances on wheels with doorstops, or
  remove or lock their wheels to prevent them from roll-
  ing. Cabinetry around a built-in refrigerator will prevent it from moving any direction except forward.

The Bedroom.

Chances are that an earthquake will strike when you're
in bed. It's not that earthquakes occur more often at
night—just that the odds are that you will be caught
wherever you spend the most time, and on an hours-per-
week basis, that's probably your bed.

The San Fernando quake caught my husband and me
in a bed on rollers on a bare floor. The bed rolled and
yawed like a rowboat in a hurricane, tossing us with it.
The bouncing movements along with the terrifying rumbling and crashing sounds convinced me that we were
about to die, that this was the "Big One" and we were
on a block of land breaking loose from the continent. I
was convinced that great chunks of earth with houses,
streets, and people must be falling into a churning sea.
I wanted to hold John's hand to face the experience
together, but we were being tossed around so violently
that I couldn't even touch him. When the shaking finally
stopped, it seemed as though our house was about to
collapse. The wardrobe doors had buckled—I thought the
walls had, too—and the dresser had tipped over onto the
bed. Amazingly, we were not hurt. Acting instinctively—
and wrongly—I ran to the baby's room, snatched her out
of her broken crib, and began to run outside. The ground
started shaking again. Running down the hall with our
baby in my arms was oddly like running through a car-
nival crazy house. The floor seemed to rise up to meet

my feet one minute and was lower than it was supposed to be the next. The walls kept bumping me. I wasn't sure which way was up. John followed us out, cutting his foot on some broken glass. We were very lucky, because we had done the worst thing possible during an earthquake, that is, to run outside while the ground is shaking.

Looking back, I can see that the way our bedroom was arranged exaggerated our terror as well as the danger. The bed on rollers slid easily across the bare floor with the motion of the quake, bumping the walls and producing more movement than we would otherwise have experienced. If our dresser had been any taller or heavier, it would have injured us as it fell onto the bed. A few thoughtful preparations beforehand would have eliminated most of the hazards. It still would have been terrifying, because we were experiencing forces equivalent to gravity at times, and it was impossible to control our bodies.

In readying a bedroom for an earthquake, there are three main goals: to prevent objects from falling on the bed, causing injuries; to keep the escape route clear; and to keep needed equipment accessible. Placement of the bed is the first safety consideration. Locate the bed near an interior wall, away from windows and hanging light fixtures. If the bed must be next to a window, install shatter-resistant plastic film over the glass. Be sure that the bed is not on rollers, and if it is on bare floor, use plastic non-skid coasters to reduce sliding. A waterbed will amplify the motion of a quake, but as long as you expect a wild ride, and have padded rails or an "air frame," it should be safe. Try to stay in the middle of the bed during the shaking.

Try to imagine what would happen if someone could pick up your bedroom and shake it. Loose things will jiggle, slide, or fall. Eliminate or anchor with Quake Tape or Quake Grip® such hazards as a ceramic ashtray, vase, or lamp next to your bed that could fall and break, perhaps cutting your feet or hands when you getting out of bed. The pitcher and drinking glass should be unbreakable plastic.

After an earthquake, it should be easy to find your flashlight, your glasses, your shoes (to protect your feet from broken glass), your bathrobe, and, if needed, a few days supply of essential medication. Many experts recommend keeping a pair of work gloves at the bedside too. Be sure that every member of the household above age two has a flashlight and shoes at bedside. Plan your exit routes, first assuming that you will be in bed and that it will be dark, and then considering other possibilities.

Armoires, freestanding closets, dressers, display cases, and bookcases could tip over during an earthquake unless they are securely anchored to the studs of the wall. Either bolt directly through the back of the furniture into the wall studs or use steel angle brackets. Fallen furnishings could block your escape route, besides causing injury and damage.

Check the upper shelves of your closets for heavy items, which might slide off. Store your heavy items on the floor or low shelves. Lighter items such as pillows and blankets can be safely stored up high. Cupboards should be closed with earthquake latches.

Figure 5-9. So many furnishings and books fell to the floor in this room during the 1971 San Fernando earthquake that the door was blocked. (Photo by Mavis Shafer.)

Figure 5-10. Bookshelves and other tall furniture should be attached to the wall by bolts, hinges, wire, or hooks. A guard rail will help prevent objects from sliding off open shelves.

The Bathroom.

The primary danger in the bathroom during an earthquake is broken glass. Mirrors, toiletries, and medicines can fall and break. More and more personal care products

are packaged in plastic now, but liquid medicines, per-
fume, cologne, and after-shave lotion are sometimes supplied in glass containers. Select products in unbreakable
containers when possible, and dispose of unneeded
bottles and jars. Be sure to use only unbreakable containers in the shower and bathtub, because you could be
cut by the broken glass.

The door on your medicine cabinet can be secured by
a child-proof latch. If it is not secure, do not store any
thing fragile or breakable in it. Only towels and other
lightweight and shatterproof items should be kept on
open shelves, unless they are well secured as described
above. Cleaning supplies in the bathroom should be
stored on the bottom shelf of a low cabinet, closed with
an earthquake-proof latch.

Newer shower doors and tub enclosures are made of
tempered glass, which shatters into lots of small harm-
less pieces, or sticky, unbreakable plastic. Old shower
doors and tub enclosures may be made of regular glass,
which could break into sharp, dangerous pieces. These
old doors should be replaced.

The Living Room, Den, and Dining Room.

To get these rooms ready for an earthquake, try to
visually shake each room. Tall furniture will probably tip
or fall; the television, VCR, stereo, speakers, lamps, and
other loose objects will also slide or fall. Chandeliers and
heavy lamps will swing or fall; modular units may
separate, tip, or collapse.

From the standpoint of personal safety, tall furniture,
bookcases, and chandeliers pose the greatest danger in
an earthquake. The most dangerous is the typical student's bookcase or shelf unit put together with bricks or
blocks and boards. The various parts, some heavy, some
light, are not tied together, so they are likely to pull apart
and fall, dropping whatever books and other things are
on the shelves. This type of bookcase should be dis-
mantled and replaced immediately. Stacked cubes or

other modular units may be almost as dangerous unless they are anchored, tied together, and cross-braced.

Bookcases, entertainment centers, china cabinets, grandfather clocks, and other tall furniture should be bolted to the studs of the wall behind them by bolting directly through the back of the furniture or by using three-inch steel angle brackets with two bolts into the furniture, and two bolts into the studs. Plumber's tape (perforated steel) can also be used for certain situations. Remember to use oversized steel hardware so that the connection will be strong. Free standing bookshelves should be bolted to the floor and to ceiling joists or overhead steel bracing. Adjustable shelves, the boards which rest on wall brackets, can be stabilized with clips or wire to connect the board to the bracket.

Bookcases that are anchored or braced at the top are less likely to sway enough to empty onto the floor, but a wire or wooden fence should be added to each shelf of books for protection. Other items stored on open shelves can be anchored with fishing line, VelcroQuake Tape®, silicon adhesive or hardware.

Figure 5-11. The home entertainment center fell onto the sofa and chair during the Morgan Hill earthquake. (Photo courtesy Bill Gates.)

Chandeliers and other hanging objects should be securely attached to the ceiling joists or to a strong board attached to the top of the joists.

Paintings and mirrors often drop during earthquakes. Be sure that the hardware, both for the wall and for the object to be hung, as well as the wire, is strong enough to support the weight of the painting or mirror, including the weight of the frame, and that the object is secured to the studs of the wall. Security hangers or anti-theft devices, available at picture frame dealers, will prevent framed pictures from falling during an earthquake. The Velcro and Quake Tape® will help stabilize hanging pictures, too.

Lamps often tip over during earthquakes, because of their high center of gravity. Once they begin to tip or wobble with the action of the earthquake, they often fall over. Select lamps with broad bases and low centers of gravity, and place them on sturdy tables. All the objects on tables and open shelves can slide or "walk" during earthquake shaking. Vases, art objects, and other small items should not be placed near the edges of tables. These objects can be secured as described.

Windows.

Large windows, particularly next to exits and beds or other places where people spend a lot of time, can be dangerous if they break during an earthquake. There are two options: tempered glass, which breaks into tiny rounded pieces, or shatter-resistant film, a plastic film applied to glass. The film is less expensive than replacing the glass, but it must be installed by an expert. The shatter-resistant film is similar to the film that may tint windows or make them reflective, but the plastic and the adhesive is stronger so that if the window breaks, the plastic holds the pieces together.

The Laundry Room, Utility Room, Garage, and Workshop.

With its high center of gravity, the home appliance, which is most vulnerable to earthquake damage, is the standard water heater. Although modern water heaters have been designed to be a bit more steady than the early models, these large water-filled cylinders are still likely to "walk" or even tip over during an earthquake. If this happens, the utility lines may be disconnected, causing gas or water leakage, or electrical shorts, fires, or explosions. And if it does tip over, you could lose one of your best sources of drinking water for the period following the earthquake.

To prevent the water heater from moving or tipping over, wrap it with two metal straps, near the top and bottom. Use perforated metal tape (plumber's tape), and loop it all around the heater before bolting the ends to the studs of the wall. Use four-inch lag bolts with washers. Make sure that the metal tape is pulled taut. For added security, install a plywood "shelf" behind the heater, cut to fit the water heater's circular shape, or a two-by-four or similar board behind the heater to prevent it from tipping. (See illustration.) Flexible gas lines should be used for the water heater, and for other gas appliances.

Careful storage of flammable, poisonous, and explosive substances may prevent injury, fire, and other damage. Paint, gasoline, paint thinner, bleach, ammonia, pesticides, herbicides, and other dangerous products should be stored in unbreakable, clearly identified containers. These should be stored in low cupboards with earthquake-proof latches. Check these cupboards periodically to eliminate any unnecessary hazards. For example, the advantages of keeping a can of gasoline on hand may not outweigh the risk of its constant presence.

Volatile substances—gasoline, paint, or lacquer thinner, etc.—should not be stored in a room with a pilot light. They should be carefully stored in a well-ventilated room equipped with a fire extinguisher.

Lumber, heavy cans of paint, or tools stored on open shelves above your car in the garage or in the garage rafters may fall onto you or your car during an earthquake. The fallen objects may prevent access to your car.

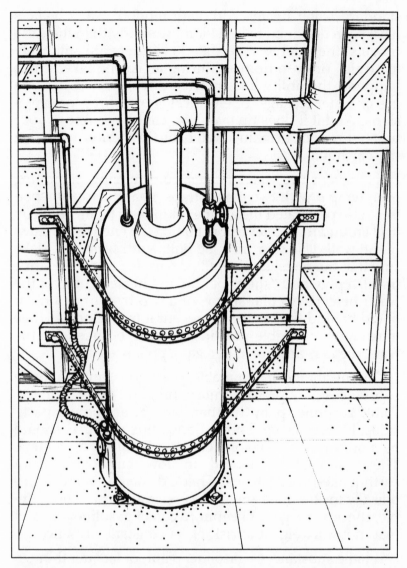

Figure 5-12. Secure the water heater to the studs of the wall with steel belts.

Workshops and work areas should be arranged for earthquake safety as well as convenience. Install fences or doors on open shelves. If you keep lumber or firewood, stack it in a sturdy crib no higher than waist level.

Figure 5-13. Gasoline, paint thinner, and other dangerous products should be stored on lower shelves and secured with a protective bar, as shown. If there are children around, hazardous products should be kept in locked cabinets.

PREPARING THE WORKPLACE

The Office.

Office furniture presents both protection and hazards to the occupants. Most desks in offices are strong, and offer good protection to people who crawl under them. Photographs of offices after damaging earthquakes usually show filing cabinets, bookcases, light fixtures, and other debris that has fallen on desks, so plan to get under the desk quickly.

Filing cabinets, partitions, bookshelves, and steel storage units can tip over unless they are bolted to the wall. Use three-inch steel angle brackets to bolt the units to the studs of the wall. Bolting filing cabinets together also increases their stability. Be sure that the drawers on filing cabinets lock when they are closed, because as the drawer slides open during an earthquake, it can injure someone. Use wire or plumber's tape to "fence" books and other items on open shelves. Don't keep potted plants, vases, or other heavy objects on high shelves. Typewriters, computers, telephones, and other office equipment can be secured with Velcro Quake Grip® or other desktop anchoring system.

The Warehouse.

Tall racks of stored equipment and supplies pose a great danger in an earthquake. I have been in many warehouses with free standing shelves holding thousands of supplies ten or more feet high. These shelves should be bolted to the floor and further anchored with steel channel bars to the upper walls. Goods should be stored carefully, with the heavier items down low. Removable fences can prevent the items from sliding off the shelves, while still allowing access to workers and forklifts.

Great care should be taken when storing chemicals or other potentially hazardous materials. Drums piled one on top of another are very dangerous, and should be stored on shelves with fences. Incompatible materials stored close together could mix in a spill. Chemistry and test laboratories should store their chemicals by type instead of alphabetically, making sure that each container is secured—while in use and when stored.

Company Plans.

Businesses with only a few employees can make plans similar to a family's. All companies have an obligation to their employees to maintain a disaster plan. An emergency evacuation area must be designated, a nearby safe place, usually outdoors, where workers can get together after a fire or earthquake. If outdoors, it should be out in the open, away from buildings or power lines. If there is no open space nearby, an underground parking area or other secure place can be designated, but remember that parked cars can bounce around during earthquakes, so people shouldn't plan to stand or sit between parked cars. Sitting in a parked car should be safe, however. Set up a procedure to account for all employees. Plan and post evacuation routes and alternate routes, and keep them clear. Plan assistance for people with disabilities, both employees and people who may be visiting or conducting business. Conduct regular evacuation drills.

Assign and train teams of employees to handle first aid, sweep and rescue, fire response, evacuation, damage assessment, and security. Train all employees in fire and earthquake preparedness, identifying places of safety at work. Appoint and train floor wardens to take leadership in emergencies.

Reduce the risk of non-structural damage by securing furnishings and stored goods. Anticipate power outages and plan appropriate lighting and computer security. Stock appropriate supplies and equipment (listed in Chapter 4 and this chapter), addressing the possibility that employees may not be able to leave for up to seventy-two hours, and that there may be customers or visitors trapped as well.

Figure 5-14. The 1989 Loma Prieta earthquake caused severe damage to businesses in Santa Cruz, CA. (Photo courtesy Richard Holden)

HIGH-RISE BUILDINGS

Most of the guidelines for earthquake preparation in other buildings also apply to high-rises, but there are some differences that will be important to you if you live, work, or spend any time in or near tall buildings.

When a high-rise building is designed without earthquake protection, the stresses considered are mainly vertical; that is, the building is designed to withstand its own weight as well as the weight of the contents, and hold up against wind. Earthquake engineering adds other dimensions, because the building must be able to hold together as it is shaken from side to side and up and down. The roof can't just rest on top of the walls; the roof and walls must be tied together so that the walls do not pull apart and allow the roof to fall. Newer multi-story buildings in seismically active areas have been designed to be flexible while holding together. To dissipate the force of the ground shaking through a tall structure, the building is designed to sway as a unit in a side-to-side motion. Without this planned flexibility, the various elements of a large building would move at different rates, creating additional stresses within the building that could weaken it to the point of collapse.

Besides engineering for earthquake resistance, the nature and quality of materials contribute to a building's performance during an earthquake. Concrete, if used, must be reinforced with steel, and the structural steel must be of high tensile strength. Workmanship is another important factor, particularly in the joining together of concrete sections. Tight building schedules may lead to neglect of important details which might weaken the structure. The building code sets minimum standards for construction, and requires inspection at designated stages. As previously discussed, these standards cannot be ignored, but they may be exceeded; that is, a building may be designed to be much stronger than the code requires. The building inspector is expected to be both honest and qualified to evaluate the structural engineering of modern buildings, but in understaffed offices or "boom town" situations, these criteria are not always met. Part of the damage to Alaskan buildings in the 1964 earthquake was attributed to sloppy workmanship, which was not caught by inspection.

Figure 5-15. The top four floors of the Mansion Charaima Apartment Building in Caracas, Venezuela, collapsed during the earthquake of July 29, 1967. (Photo courtesy NOAA/EDS.)

Figure 5-16. The 1985 Mexico City earthquake caused the total collapse of a twenty-one story steel-frame office building. Most high-rise buildings perform well in earthquakes. (Photo courtesy National Geophysical Data Center.)

Unfortunately, when we work or live in a high-rise building, most of us have no way of determining how well it has been designed, engineered, or constructed. We should be aware, however, that no high-rise building has been designed to go through a large earthquake without any damage. The usual procedure is to design a building to withstand the largest earthquake expected in that area, based on records of previous earthquakes, with total anticipated damage below ten percent of the building's cost, and with that damage limited to non-structural elements such as plaster, glass, non-bearing walls, etc. If such a goal is reached, the building can be repaired following an earthquake, and it would still be earthquake resistant. Sometimes a designer will even *plan* the failure of a non-bearing wall or window wall as a means of dissipating horizontal energy without structural damage to the building. The philosophy is sometimes described: "In a moderate earthquake, no damage. In a great earthquake, no death."

The key here is to *expect* windows to break, and plaster and suspended ceilings to fall during and after a large earthquake. If high-rise buildings are designed to sway, as they should, during earthquakes, unsecured objects will undoubtedly slide around inside, particularly on the upper floors. That's why it is very important to secure the furnishings of a high-rise building as previously described. Bookshelves, filing cabinets, desks, and other pieces of furniture should be anchored to the floor or wall. This will prevent them from sliding back and forth, even acting as battering rams to break through windows or walls. Carpets may help to reduce this action. Large windows above the fourth or fifth floor should have guard rails installed on the inside, and/or shatter-resistant plastic film on the glass.

Develop a plan of action in advance. Talk with your household members and/or co-workers about the possible dangers which an earthquake may pose for your particular building. If possible, talk to the building manager to plan the best course of action during and after the earthquake. Follow the guidelines in Chapters 6 and 7.

Figure 5-17. The middle floors of the Hotel De Carlo failed during the 1985 Mexico City quake. This damage may have been caused by pounding from the building at the left.

MOBILE HOMES

A mobile home could be a good place to be during an earthquake—but unless it is properly set up, the unit can fall off its supports, endangering its occupants. The Santa Barbara, California earthquake of August 1978 was one of the first earthquakes to occur near large numbers of mobile homes. The most widespread residential damage caused by this moderate (M5.2) earthquake involved mobile homes. About twenty-five per cent of all the mobile units in the epicentral area were damaged. In the Santa Barbara West Mobile Home Park, more than thirty-five percent of the one-hundred and forty-seven homes were shaken off their foundations, causing damage to plumbing and utility lines, porches, stairways, skirts* and

---

Skirting is the aluminum or wooden siding which extends from the bottom of the mobile home to the ground, giving the appearance of a solid foundation, and hiding the utility connections and building supports.

awnings as well as some damage to the integrity of the structures. Four of the mobile homes in the park were so badly damaged as to be uninhabitable, and one burned to the ground because of a ruptured gas line. Experts now estimate that mobile homes are damaged about twice as much by earthquakes as wood frame homes.

What are referred to here categorically as "mobile homes" could probably be more accurately termed "manufactured" or "transportable" buildings, since these units have changed dramatically from the days of the house trailer, and are used for a variety of functions besides housing. Mobile homes frequently function as office buildings or school classrooms—and earthquakes do not distinguish between them.

Vulnerability of the mobile unit to earthquake damage is due not so much to the structure as to the way that it is set up and anchored in place. A mobile home is constructed in a factory and is towed on its own chassis in one or more parts to a location that often becomes its permanent residence. Once it is installed somewhere, it usually stays where it is—unless an earthquake moves it. It can, however, be moved from one location to another if the owner so chooses.

In the factory, mobile homes are built on a steel underframe with assembly line techniques. Since the structure will be towed by a truck along highways at speeds up to fifty-five miles per hour, and over the same bumps, potholes, and curves on which cars are driven, the mobile home is built to be both flexible and strong to absorb the shocks of transportation. Riding on its inflated tires, the unit usually survives the trip without damage. Earthquake forces may be different from travel stresses, however, and some critics urge simulated tests and studies to evaluate the performance of mobile home construction under earthquake conditions.

Once it reaches its destination, the home may be lifted onto a solid foundation and be attached to it, or it may be jacked up and left resting on slender supports, which stand on the ground. Frequently, the axle and wheels are

Figure 5-18. These steps used to lead up to the front door of the mobile home, which fell off its foundation in Morgan Hill, California. (Photo courtesy Bill Gates.)

Figure 5-19. The Morgan Hill earthquake damaged the gas line to this mobile home, which was destroyed by the resulting explosion and fire. (Photo courtesy Bill Gates.)

removed, leaving the heavy structure perched precariously on a series of concrete or steel pedestals. In some cases, the pedestals are nothing more than stacks of cinder blocks. If the unit has been set up in this fashion, the rocking back and forth of earthquake action can topple the supports and allow the structure to fall.

Specialized earthquake stabilizing devices for mobile homes are available now, and the California Department of Housing and Community Development certifies them. These devices have proved to be effective in preventing or minimizing damage in several recent earthquakes.

Besides the approved safety devices, there are several ways to plan for greater earthquake stability in mobile homes. J.S. Barish, a structural engineer retained by the California Seismic Safety Commission, advises that wheels, inflated tires, and axles can be a definite safety factor during an earthquake.

These four precautions will improve the earthquake preparedness of a mobile home:

1. Keep the axle, wheels, and inflated tires on the unit.
2. Reduce interior hazards in the same way as for conventional housing. (See "Preparing every room" in this chapter.)
3 Install an earthquake safety device to keep the unit from falling off its supports.
4. Install an automatic gas shutoff valve.

Part III

During and After the Earthquake

6

What To Do
During An Earthquake

The usual advice about what to do when a good-sized earthquake strikes is to stay calm. That's good advice, but it isn't easy to follow. Years ago, a well known geologist's advice was to stand still, count to forty, and then it wouldn't matter what you did. I think he must have been only half-serious; if things are falling on top of you, you'd better try to move.

If it's the "Big One," and you're close to it, don't worry about doing the right thing. You won't be able to run outside (wrong) or drop under a table or desk (right), because the earthquake will be in control of the situation. When the shaking stops, there may be a few seconds or even minutes before another shock, and that's the time to react appropriately by moving to a safe spot nearby. This is also the time when your advance planning may pay off, depending on where you are and just how big the earthquake really is.

There's a chance, when a big earthquake hits, that you may have a few seconds between the realization that *"this is it . . . an earthquake!"* and the time when the shaking takes control of you. During these few seconds, move to the closest safe place. In a smaller earthquake, or some distance from the epicenter of a big one, you will be able to move to a safe place while the ground is actually shaking. Staying calm and avoiding panic during an earthquake are the words of advice most often given, and for good reason.

117

Don't Run Outside During an Earthquake.

Photographs of severe earthquake damage almost always show piles of rubble all around buildings. There are many documented cases of serious injuries and deaths being caused by people who run outdoors during an earthquake. Before you expose yourself to the risk of being hit with falling debris, you should be positive that you will be in more danger staying inside, and this is very rarely the case. When people try to run during an earthquake, they often fall or bump into things, even if they don't get hit on the head by falling objects.

I think that most people are either "runners" or "freezers" when it comes to a frightening earthquake or any other seemingly lifethreatening situation. I'm the type who freezes, who probably wouldn't even be able to run out of the path of a speeding car. I'd just freeze, rooted to the ground, unable to move. The "runners," on the other hand, take off running when they recognize danger. Both types need to overcome their initial response to in an earthquake in order to move *quickly and carefully* to the closest safe place.

If you know what to do, and others around you are frightened, tell them what to do. We advise teachers to immediately start shouting commands to their students: "Drop! Get down! Get under cover! Hold on! Stay down!" and to continue shouting appropriate commands until the shaking stops.

They will need to shout because earthquakes are so noisy, and the constant stream of directions keeps them somewhat in control of the situation. It gives teachers and students the impression that this is something that they can handle, so panic is less likely. The same will be true for adults. If you know what to do, your calm, positive attitude can inspire confidence and prevent the tragic accidents that often result from panic.

CHOOSING APPROPRIATE ACTION

Take Cover in the Closest Safe Place.

Your most immediate concern will be to protect yourself from things that may fall on top of you, whether it's broken glass or a whole building. Frank Carbonara, who survived the collapse of the San Fernando Veterans Administration Hospital in the 1971 San Fernando earthquake, crawled under a kitchen sink, as the building was collapsing. He had to wait fifty-eight hours to be rescued, but his quick thinking saved his life.

Once you are in your safe place, stay there. Earthquakes seldom last longer than a minute, but it can seem like much longer. Stay where you are until the ground stops shaking and things stop falling.

Drop!

Earthquake drills in schools now usually begin with the teacher shouting, "Drop!" or "Duck and cover!" or "Drop and hold!" When I was in school, the "drop drills" were designed for civil defense; the idea, I think, was for us to drop before bombs were dropped on us. It wouldn't have done us much good, but the drills now do a terrific job of teaching young people what to do during an earthquake. "Duck and cover!" means the same thing, but adds the important message of getting under cover, as under a desk. "Drop and hold!" adds another important concept, that of holding onto whatever is above you.

The "drop" position is on your hands and knees, making yourself into a little ball—well, maybe not so little, but small enough to fit under a table or desk. Hide your eyes in the crook of your elbow to protect them from broken glass. Use your other hand to hold onto the table leg or the side of the desk. The furniture might be sliding, and holding on will make sure that you keep the protection above you. Crawl along with it, if you must. Another safe position under furniture is actually sitting under the furniture, leaving both hands free to hold onto the desk or table leg.

The drop position under a chair or between rows of chairs is also safe during an earthquake. In schools, some 'desks' are actually chairs with a writing surface on one armrest. High school and college students can't actually fit under these desks, yet they are protected by the rows of desks. In auditoriums and theaters, the rows of seats offer good protection, whether you are actually under the seat or just between the rows.

If you're "dropping" in a hallway, or outdoors, or next to an interior wall, or anywhere there isn't anything to hold onto, put your other hand across the back of your neck to protect it. If there is a book, pillow, jacket, or other protection at hand, hold it over your neck and head.

Doorways for Protection.

Earthquake protection experts don't always agree on some of the finer points, and a current discussion is

Figure 6-1. Bookshelves, books, and office supplies fell during the 1979 Imperial Valley earthquake. Getting under the desk or table would have protected people in this office. (Photo courtesy Bill Gates.)

underway about the safety of doorways. There's no doubt that the doorway itself is a pretty good place during an earthquake. The extra construction around the doorframe makes it one of the strongest parts of a building. In addition, there usually isn't much above a doorway to fall on a person, and most injuries are caused by falling objects. Some older buildings have transoms or air conditioning units above doors, but these are exceptions.

The biggest problem with the doorway is the door. It swings back and forth during an earthquake, and you might find yourself fighting the door as much as the earthquake, especially if it has an automatic closing device. The way to brace yourself in a doorway is to stand with your back against the hinges of the door, feet spread wide apart for balance, leaning across to hold onto the opposite side. For a short person, or in a wide doorway, this is not a very comfortable or secure position.

There have been reports of injuries caused by the door or doorknob hitting the person, while taking cover in the doorway. A woman in the 1987 Whittier Narrows earthquake reported that she braced herself in the doorway, but the door was pounding her. When she dropped to her knees, she was hit in the head by the doorknob.

Another problem with planning to take cover in the doorway is that there might be too many people for the number of doors. In work situations or other group places, if everyone dashes for the doorway, there will be injuries.

I think that we can conclude that if there's a sturdy table or desk nearby, taking cover under it would be preferable to the doorway. The ideal doorway for earthquakes would be one without a door. But if a doorway with a door is the only safe place nearby, brace yourself, try to hold off the door with your shoulder or hip, and hold on tight.

FINDING A SAFE PLACE

The safest place to take cover during the earthquake, assuming you can move, will be dependent on where you are.

Outside.

The safest place to be during an earthquake is outside in the open, on flat land, away from coastal areas, and out from under tall buildings, power lines, masonry walls, or anything else that might fall. Second base on a baseball field, for example, would be ideal.

Although large cracks in the ground have been known to open up, these are extremely rare. The old story of a crack opening up, swallowing a cow, and closing back up again, leaving nothing but her tail sticking out, has been attributed to several California quakes as well as the New Madrid, Missouri quakes of 1811-12. But there has never been any proof that this really happened. Another old story is that of the miner who was sleeping outdoors and jumped up when the 1857 Fort Tejon, California earthquake struck, and looked back to see his camping gear disappearing into the ground. These stories are remembered, because they are both colorful and rare.

Figure 6-2. The exterior walls of this unreinforced brick building collapsed onto the sidewalk during the 1971 San Fernando earthquake. (Photo courtesy Los Angeles Department of Building and Safety.)

Earthquakes do cause landslides, as was discussed earlier. If the ground is unstable, the shaking can cause it to give way and slide or slump. Sometimes rocks or boulders break loose from hillsides during earthquakes and roll downhill. Beaches and low-lying coastal areas, including lakeshores, are not safe places during earthquakes because of the danger of tsunamis or seiches.

If you are outside when the earthquake strikes, move to the safest place nearby, away from tall buildings and overhead wires, and "drop," sit, or lie down until the ground stops shaking. Don't go indoors during the shaking unless you are on a sidewalk or street below tall buildings, which might be dropping broken glass and other debris. In that case, duck into the closest doorway.

In A Car.

A car is a pretty good place to be during an earthquake, as long as it isn't under a bridge or something else that could fall on top of it. If you are driving when an earthquake starts, slow down carefully and come to a stop by the side of the road, but not under power lines, street lamps, bridges, or tall buildings, if possible. If you are on a bridge, keep driving slowly until you and the cars behind are off, and then stop. Stay in the car with your seatbelt buckled.

The car may shake like crazy, but it probably won't tip over if it's on flat ground. If a wire falls on top of your car, be very careful. Assume that it is live, and roll up all windows immediately. Live wires jump around, and you don't want one coming through the window.

At Home.

Home is a good place to be during an earthquake, especially if you have eliminated the hazards and secured all the emergency supplies. The chances are good that your house, condominium, or apartment building won't collapse. A single story building almost never collapses

Figure 6-3. Television sets crashed to the floor during the 1987 Whittier Narrows earthquake. (Photo courtesy Bill Gates.)

during an earthquake, unless it was built of unreinforced bricks or rocks, and two or three-story buildings rarely collapse either. Your main danger at home will be falling objects and fire.

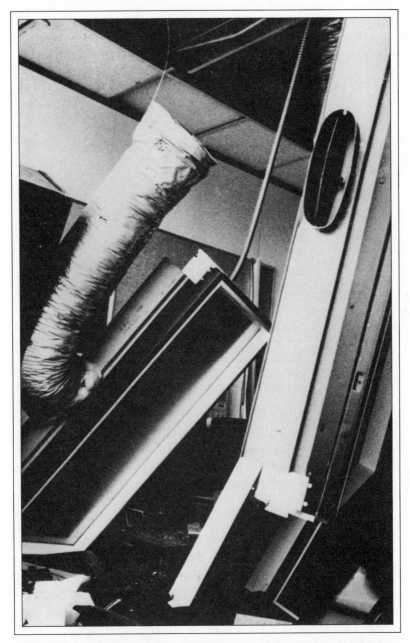

Figure 6-4. Lighting fixtures and an air duct fell onto this desk during the 1979 Imperial Valley earthquake. The closest place of safety was under the desk. (Photo courtesy Bill Gates.)

Figure 6-5. Merchandise was shaken from the shelves of this Commerce City, Colorado, market by the earthquake of November 26, 1967. (Photo courtesy The Denver Post.)

If you can, duck under a piece of sturdy furniture and hold on, or find another safe place as described earlier. If you are in bed when the earthquake begins, and if you have made sure that nothing will fall on your bed, stay there.

In A Public Building.

Stay where you are and assess the situation. In most public places, the best thing to do during an earthquake is to stay where you are and drop. In a restaurant, get under the table. In a theater, stadium, or amphitheater, drop between the rows of seats.

If you are in a store, shopping mall, or a place where people are standing or walking, stand still to see what the other people do. If you must move, do so slowly. Try to find a wall or other protection to lean against. In any emergency in a crowded place, there are dangers of pushing and trampling, and if the lights are off, the situation will be worse. Try to stay out of the way of the crowd. Stores and other public buildings are required to clearly identify emergency exits. Train yourself to notice the location of these exits before there is trouble.

In the supermarket or other store, goods are bound to be falling all around you during an earthquake. The worst places to be in a grocery store are near the soft drinks, liquor, or the cleaning supplies because of the dangers of broken glass, spilled chemicals, and exploding pressurized cans. If you are pushing a shopping cart, use it for protection. Drop and hold onto the cart.

At Work.

In an office building, the safest place is usually under a desk. File cabinets, bookshelves, and other tall office furniture could tip over easily during earthquakes. Look around ahead of time to identify other places of protection such as hallways and interior walls where nothing can fall on you.

Industrial buildings offer the additional hazards of heavy equipment and supplies. Warehouses often store heavy supplies on tall, free-standing steel shelves; the shelves and the supplies may both fall. Additionally, materials used in production and research laboratories can be extremely hazardous if spilled, and combinations of chemicals can be deadly. Again, try to locate safe places in advance, and talk to your employer about safe storage of materials and other non-structural hazard reductions.

In A High-Rise Building.

Tall buildings sway back and forth during earthquakes, so you'll need to hold on while the ground shakes. Again, the trick is to find the closest safe place and hold on tight.

Take cover under a desk or table unless it's right by a low window. Turn away from the windows. Hold on and move along with the desk as it slides. Or brace yourself in the central hallway or against an interior wall. If you are in a stairwell, sit down and hold on. Stay out of the elevators. If you are in an elevator, step out of it if the door is open. Otherwise, use the drop position.

MAKING TOUGH DECISIONS

You might compare these rules to seatbelts in your car; seatbelts will protect almost everyone in a car accident, but once in a while, the seatbelt itself could make the injuries worse. Sometimes breaking the rules about earthquake safety is the best thing to do at that time and place. We know that running outside of a building, while the ground is shaking, is dangerous, but once in a very great while, running outside will turn out to be the right thing to do.

It seems to me that the best way to protect yourself is to gain an understanding about earthquakes and their effects. Then make your plans, stock your supplies, and reduce as many hazards as you can. At that point, you can forget all about earthquakes until you feel the ground under you begin to shake. Then, look around, decide what is best to do where you are, and quickly move to the safest place nearby.

7

What To Do Afterwards

SETTING PRIORITIES

The top priorities following a damaging earthquake are human safety and extinguishing or preventing fires. If two capable adults are present, one should check for injuries and establish priorities for medical attention, while the other checks for fires. If there are more adults to help and a large area to check, they should work in twos, threes, or fours, systematically dividing the area to be covered.

In a workplace or public building, there may be teams assigned to first aid, sweep and rescue, fire response, and evacuation. If that is the case, cooperate with the teams and follow their directions. Unfortunately, relatively few businesses have developed and maintained good disaster response plans, but if you are lucky enough to be in a well-prepared facility, then you must do your part.

As human beings, we have a responsibility to our community and other people. We have to take care of one another. Most people who are caught in a crisis react very well. Those who know what to do can guide the others. Don't be afraid to give orders. You may be the only one who knows what to do, and the presence of a responsible person will have a calming effect on people who are injured or frightened.

This chapter will attempt to cover most of the conditions we might experience immediately after an earthquake, and will attempt to prioritize the steps to take.

ATTENDING TO INJURIES

First, check yourself for injuries, applying first aid and protecting yourself with shoes and gloves. Then, make sure that the people around you are safe and don't require *immediate* attention. Check to see if each victim is breathing and look for profuse bleeding. Obviously, these situations demand immediate action. Control the bleeding, and if the person is not breathing, check to see that the airway is open, and then check for heartbeat. Cardiopulmonary resuscitation is used when there is no heartbeat and no breathing, but you must have had training to administer CPR. If there is a heartbeat, mouth-to-mouth or mouth-to-nose resuscitation may help the victim start breathing again.

Once the critical injuries are stabilized, check for fires and potential fires (as detailed in the following section), or make sure that someone else is doing so, and then return to the injured.

Some injuries may be aggravated by moving the victim, and you may be faced with some difficult decisions. Don't move an injured person, even a short distance, even to turn him or her over, unless you absolutely must for a compelling safety reason, such as a fire nearby. Your first-aid class will have prepared you to move a victim with as little further injury as possible.

If the building is secure—no fires, leaking gas, spilled chemicals, or serious damage to the structure of the building—you should keep injured people where they are. Stabilize the injuries and treat for shock; try to secure professional help for the seriously injured.

After you have noted the victim's breathing and heartbeat, and controlled any profuse bleeding, carefully check, by observation and touching, for broken bones and other wounds. Observe the victim's general appearance, noting skin pallor or discoloration, sweaty or dry skin, consciousness, drowsiness, ability to answer questions, and size and reactiveness of the pupils of the eyes. Loosen any constricting clothing. Try to maintain the normal body temperature and cover with a blanket. If you are in doubt about what is wrong and don't see any obvious injuries, look for evidence such as broken glass and fallen objects, which might indicate the cause of injury. Look for emergency information on a bracelet or necklace, or in the victim's wallet.

Try to look and sound calm around injured people. Act like everything is under control, even if it isn't. If possible, check a first-aid manual (there should be one in your first-aid kit) to be sure of using the best treatment. The victim's condition may change, so continue to observe the physical and mental state of the injured. Listlessness and unresponsiveness could be as much an indication of trouble as hysteria. If possible, stay with the victim until help arrives. If you must leave, assign someone else the responsibility of caring for the injured.

FIRES AND FIRE HAZARDS

After checking for and treating critical injuries, the next important concern is the possibility of fires and potential fires. If possible, one person or group should attend to injuries while another immediately checks for fires. Don't light matches or candles. Leaking natural gas and spilled flammable products can be ignited by flames, pilot lights, or electrical shorts.

If you smell gas or have reason to suspect that gas lines may be broken—because you see a toppled appliance or hear gas leaking, for example—immediately go outside to turn off the main gas line at the meter. Leave the gas turned off until a gas company serviceperson can assist you.

If a gas line has ruptured outside, beyond the meter, you won't be able to shut it off. The strong smell should alert you to evacuate the area and call the fire department, if possible. Remember that gas is very explosive, so keep all flames and sparks away from it. If the leaking gas is already burning, though, it won't explode.

If your electrical lines are sparking or crackling, turn off all individual circuit breakers and the main switch at the service panel. If water is leaking from broken pipes or fixtures, turn off the water main by turning it clockwise.

If fires have already started, try to notify the fire department, evacuate the building, and, if possible, extinguish the fire. Fires demand both speed and judgment. If the quake has damaged your local fire station or started many fires, there may be no speedy assistance available; if the telephone lines are out, there may be no quick way to summon help anyway. At worst, a fire may be so large that your home and others nearby may burn without your being able to do anything about it. At best, your advance preparation will have prevented fires, or your speedy action will have put them out.

If water lines have ruptured, there may be no water pressure, and you will be forced to rely upon extinguishers, baking soda, sand, or dirt. You may be able to utilize water from swimming pools, water heaters, or toilet tanks by using buckets or soaking towels and blankets.

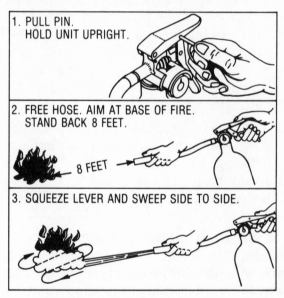

Figure 7-1. Use the PASS method to put out a fire. (Courtesy Walter Kidde.)

In any case, remember to place human safety—your own and that of others—before protection of property.

Before operating a fire extinguisher, it is important to protect human life by evacuating everyone from the fire area and closing the door behind you. Next, call for help and/or sound an alarm. Then, use your extinguisher *if it is safe to do so.* Fire departments recommend that you use the PASS method to operate your extinguisher (Pull, Aim, Squeeze, and Sweep). While holding it in a vertical position, Pull the top ring/pin out. Aim the extinguisher hose/nozzle at the *base* of the fire, Squeeze down on the trigger, and Sweep the base of the fire from side to side until the fire, or your extinguisher, is out. Finally, total evacuation will be necessary if you are unsuccessful.

AFTERSHOCKS

Damaging earthquakes are always followed by aftershocks, and some moderate earthquakes have been followed by larger earthquakes. When you feel an earthquake, there is no way to tell if it is a foreshock to a larger quake or the largest one in the sequence.

Most often, however, quakes that follow a large one are of diminishing magnitude. Sometimes, but not always, earthquakes are preceded by foreshocks. At this time, scientists can't tell until later, by viewing the completed pattern, whether the first quake is just a foreshock for a larger quake or the main shock in a sequence. After a period of seismic activity, they can look back and identify the pattern of foreshocks, main shock, and aftershocks. But immediately after a moderate earthquake, no one can tell for sure if the next quake will be smaller or larger. Sometimes major earthquakes come as a series of two or three or even more large jolts.

In general, if you've felt a moderate earthquake, be alert for more earthquakes to follow. As you go through the recovery period, be prepared for another earthquake at any minute, and take cover in the closest safe place every time the ground shakes.

SPECIFIC PLACES AND SITUATIONS

At Home.

Your priorities at home are basically the same as anywhere else. If you are barefoot, put on shoes before you walk anywhere after an earthquake. Follow the standard procedures by checking yourself and the other family members for injuries, treating serious conditions promptly. Then, quickly check for fires, potential fires, and serious damage. Put out fires and turn off the gas if you smell it leaking.

Unless there are known hazards outdoors, or medical or other conditions that would make evacuation unwise or uncomfortable, take the family to the outdoor evacuation area to wait for aftershocks and damage information. This is not essential, but many people feel more comfortable outdoors after an earthquake, because it is usually the safest place, and, if a large aftershock or a larger earthquake should strike, you would be protected. Depending on the size of the earthquake and your evacuation conditions, staying outdoors for several hours or longer may be a good idea.

Carefully inspect the interior and exterior of the building, checking the chimney from a distance first. Look for cracks in the walls, shifted posts or pillars, and cracks in porches and sidewalks. If you see anything other than minor cracks, evacuate the building immediately and stay out until it has been inspected for safety by a professional. Notify your local building and safety department to request an inspection.

Once your home and family are secure, check with your neighbors to see if they need assistance. Be sure to check on those who have special concerns such as pregnancy, an infant, disability or medical condition.

In An Apartment.

Large apartment complexes should have a disaster response plan similar to a large business. Smaller buildings will probably react in the same way as a neighborhood. If you evacuate, you will be going to an emergency assembly area. There, check with your neighbors to be sure that they are all safe. If necessary, set up a first aid station at the evacuation area. Share resources and plan together.

Away from Home.

If you are in your car, at a movie or store, or someplace where you do not have assurance that you will be safe, you will probably try to go home. Stay where you are for a while and wait for aftershocks and information on the radio. Remember that aftershocks, particularly the ones right after a big earthquake, can cause a lot of damage. Highway overpasses and bridges might survive the main shock, but fall during an aftershock.

After an earthquake that causes damage, drive only if you are away from tall buildings and bridges, and then your driving should be only to safety or to render assistance. The roads should be kept open for emergency vehicles. You may not be able to drive anyway. The streets could be blocked with debris, making it impossible to pass.

If a wire has fallen on your car, you must assume that it is "live," and roll up your windows immediately. The usual advice in this situation is to wait for help. If it doesn't look like help will be forthcoming, and your engine is already going, try to drive out from under the wire or around the debris. The other option is to jump out of your car, making sure that you don't touch the ground and the car at the same time. This is very important, because if the wire is live, and you touch the ground and the car, the electrical current would run through you, causing electrocution. Fortunately, it is fairly unusual for wires to fall onto cars.

Evaluate your situation. Do you think that you will be able to drive home? How far is it to walk? Are you physically capable of making the hike? Are you wearing shoes to protect your feet during a long walk over broken glass or other debris? Listen to the radio for reports of damage. Will you be walking into the hardest hit area? Is there somewhere closer that you could go for help, such as the home of a friend?

If you do reach home some time after a damaging earthquake, don't rush inside. First, look at the building from a distance, looking for signs of damage. If it looks okay, then walk around it, making a careful inspection. Don't go near the chimney. If it still looks undamaged, open the door and stand back for a few minutes. If you smell gas, leave the door open and turn the gas off at the outside meter. If you don't smell gas at first, carefully step inside and repeat the procedure.

Make a careful inspection of the inside, looking for sparking lines or other damage. My neighbor returned home after the Whittier Narrows earthquake and found her rug smoldering from a lamp that had fallen and shorted out. It hadn't burst into flames yet, but it would have if she hadn't arrived.

Figure 7-2. This older home was damaged in the 1987 Whittier Narrows earthquake. (Photo courtesy American Red Cross.)

If Separated from Your Loved One.

One of the most frightening aspects of an earthquake is not being near the ones you love. If your children are at school, for example, you will have to trust that they are safe and will be kept safe until you or someone you've designated arrives to pick them up. If husband and wife are separated, they will each try to reach their agreed upon reunion place (usually home), but they won't drop everything and run. While getting home and back together may be their top priority, they will take the time to do it safely.

In Darkness.

One of the most frightening possibilities is being caught in total darkness during and after an earthquake. Unfortunately, this isn't impossible. Many buildings don't have natural light and don't have emergency lighting either. The emergency lights or generator could also be damaged by an earthquake.

If you find yourself alone in the dark after an earthquake, take a few moments to recall the location of exits and the layout of the building. Plan your escape route, and then go slowly, using your hands to guide you. If you heard the sound of breaking glass during the earthquake, wrap your hands with a jacket or other material to protect them. Carefully move toward an exit, taking cover or "dropping" with each aftershock. Be alert for the smells of smoke or leaking gas. Go outdoors, well away from the building, and plan your strategy carefully. If you smelled leaking gas, turn off the gas at the meter. If you can't turn off the gas, try to get help.

In darkness with other people, the strategy would be essentially the same, but the first thing to do is to call to one another to find out who is present, and if anyone is hurt. If no immediate first aid is required, move together, join hands, and let the person most familiar with the building act as leader. After a recent Guatemalan earthquake, a blind person led the sighted out of a darkened building.

At Work.

If you are at work during an earthquake, check for injuries, fires, and potential fires as described above. If no disaster response teams have been assigned, assign or divide into teams to handle search and rescue, fire, and first aid. If you are not needed on a team, and if the earthquake was large enough to have caused damage or started fires, consider going carefully to the emergency assembly area.

Unless there is a fire, chemical spill, or structural damage, *do not* evacuate high-rise buildings or other buildings where the evacuation process could be hazardous or where the only assembly area would be in a place where glass from tall buildings or other debris might fall on you.

If an emergency assembly area has not been designated, it should be a nearby place out in the open where nothing can fall on people. This is frequently a parking lot, but away from parked cars, which might be bounced around in another earthquake, or a nearby park. At the assembly area, count or take roll to make sure that no one is missing. Sit down, turn on the portable radio, and wait for the disaster teams to report.

The search and rescue team goes through the entire building (large buildings require several teams), searching for trapped people by calling, looking, and lifting debris. They will check everywhere, including restrooms and storerooms. If equipped properly, they will wear hardhats, and carry crowbars, flashlights, and walkie-talkies. If they find injured people, they will call the first aid team to assist the victims.

The fire team makes a quick sweep of the building looking for fires, sparking electrical lines, spilled chemicals and leaking gas. If necessary, they will put out fires with extinguishers and turn off utilities. The facilities team assesses damage and assists the fire team with protecting the building and its occupants.

A large, well-coordinated disaster response plan includes a chain of command, with one person overall in charge. That leader will receive reports from all teams, assess the situation, and issue the evacuation order, if necessary, and other directions. If the building has been evacuated, no one will be permitted to re-enter the building until a facilities team has made a very careful inspection of the building, inside and outside, for structural damage. If the structure has been damaged, it will be sealed off until a professional inspector declares it to be safe.

Large companies will set up a roll sheet to list all those present, keep track of any serious injuries and where victims were sent, and for people to sign when leaving. Employees will be encouraged to stay there until the situation has been evaluated. There may be good reasons for staying until a trip home can be made safely.

In An Elevator.

There are few situations we can imagine that would be worse than being trapped in an elevator after an earthquake. Yet this is more common than we might think. High-rise buildings often have ten or twenty, sometimes fifty elevators, and at any given moment, many, if not all, are in use. Modern elevators are equipped with telephones for help, and you should try to use the telephone. If it is working, experience shows that trapped people handle the situation better if they can talk to the emergency operator at least every five minutes.

Being trapped is an uncomfortable experience, but the odds are very good that it's just a matter of time before the power goes on and the elevator moves you to a safe place and the doors open. Don't try to get out of the elevator. Wait for help. Even if the telephone isn't working, all the elevators will be checked, and you will not be forgotten. Sit down, try to remain calm, and talk about pleasant things with the other people.

In A High-Rise.

Evacuation in a high-rise building can be very hazardous, and sometimes there are very few safe evacuation places outside of a high-rise building. For this reason, you would not plan to evacuate a high-rise right after an earthquake unless there is a fire, chemical spill, or structural damage. Remember that broken windows are not structural damage, but big cracks, especially in the superstructure, are. After checking for injuries, fires/fire hazards, and damage on your floor, your next concern will be the state of the building itself. Communication is then the biggest problem. In those buildings and businesses with comprehensive plans as described above, communication teams will handle that challenge.

Without a disaster response plan, the building security officers are usually expected to receive reports and relay instructions. If possible, report the condition on your floor to the security department, and ask about the condition of the entire building. Look out the windows on all sides, looking at your building below and above you, looking for smoke and visible damage. Look at the sidewalk and the people down below. If there are indications of a fire or other serious trouble, then carefully begin to evacuate.

Fire in A High-Rise.

If a fire starts in a high-rise building following an earthquake, it is very important to act quickly. Notify the fire department and building security officers if possible. Then attempt to extinguish the fire with extinguishers and fire hoses. If you and those around you can put the fire out, be sure that it is completely out.

Sometimes a fire flares out of control so quickly that putting it out with extinguishers would be impossible. Plastic and other synthetic decorations or furnishings can spew out thick, poisonous smoke, and you might be risking your life by stopping to fight the fire.

If such a fire ignites near you, first evacuate everyone from the immediate fire area, closing all doors behind you. Then alert people around you and (provided your building has any) pull the nearest fire alarm. If possible, try to call the Fire Department directly, and then the security office. Be prepared to follow their instructions. If you have been alerted to a fire and instructed to evacuate the building, do so as calmly and cautiously as possible.

If the stairs are free of smoke, descend carefully and go to a safe refuge. When you feel an aftershock, sit down and hold on. If the stairwell is smoky, close the door and go to a different one. Smoke rises when hot. As smoke cools (which it quickly does in high-rise hallways and stairways), it begins to stack from the floor up, displacing fresh air with highly toxic gasses. This dense, eye irritating smoke can quickly and completely restrict visibility. Entering a hallway or stairway in conditions like this can be deadly. Staying in a room full of clear air is safer than evacuating through toxic smoke.

If you must remain in your room, close as many doors as possible between you and the fire, trying to position yourself in a room with a window. If possible, call the fire department and security office, giving your location and situation. Dampen towels, sweaters, or whatever is available to place at the base of doors to block out smoke and fumes. Do not open the window, even if it isn't smoky outside. Open windows often draw smoke into and through a room instead of letting it out. Wait for assistance.

SEEKING EMERGENCY ASSISTANCE

Immediately after an earthquake, there will be no way for you to determine whether you are close to the epicenter and in the most heavily damaged area or if there are places with far more damage and injury. For this reason, you should keep the telephones free for life-threatening cases. Hang up your telephone if the earthquake knocked the receiver off the hook. If your telephone works, *don't use it unless you have an urgent need for assistance.* Then, be sure you give complete and accurate information. The lines will be overloaded. Paramedics, ambulances, and fire engines will be in short supply after a disastrous earthquake, and life-threatening emergencies should be handled first. If you need emergency assistance, and your telephones don't work, try these ideas:

1. Drive, walk, or run to the police or fire station or hospital, whichever is closest. These agencies should be able to communicate with one another, but in a widespread disaster, they may not be able to respond to your emergency.

2. If you are fortunate enough to have a "ham" radio operator nearby, radio for assistance. Again, it may take time before you can get help, especially for individual crises.

3. For a building collapse or other situation with many casualties, do something to attract the attention of a helicopter. Wave a flag; spell out SOS on lawn or driveway.

4. Ask your neighbors for assistance.

5. Do what you can to treat the problem yourself.

TAKING CARE OF THE DEAD

It is sad to consider, but there is the possibility that someone around you might be killed in an earthquake, or die despite the best efforts of those nearby. Under normal conditions, we are obligated to notify the authorities immediately if this happens. In a major disaster, however, it may not be possible to report a death or it may not be possible for the coroner to take responsibility for the body.

The general rules in this situation are to leave the body where it is unless it is necessary to move the body for rescue work or the health and safety of others. Tag or label and cover the body, keeping the personal effects with the body.

The tag or label should include the victim's name and address, the means of identification, the exact location where found, the date and time that the body was found, and the name of the person who has written the label.

Try to report the death and the location of the body to law enforcement personnel. If, after a few hours, the coroner's representative has not arrived, wrap the body in a clean sheet, if possible. Place the body in two large plastic trash bags or wrap in sheets of plastic. Continue to keep the personal effects with the labeled or tagged body. Move the body to a cool place away from insects or animals. A garage or other cool building will do if there isn't a refrigerated room available.

Again try to notify the law enforcement authorities, reporting the new location of the body. Make sure that the body is secured or protected at all times.

AFTER THE IMMEDIATE EMERGENCY

After you have treated injuries, checked for fires and other damage, and have generally stabilized your situation, try to assess the situation around you to determine what to do next. Check on your neighbors, especially the elderly and disabled.

Listen to the Radio.

Listen to your radio for evacuation orders and other information. Remember that the initial information is not necessarily accurate. There will be rumors following an earthquake, and just because you've heard something on radio or television doesn't guarantee that it's true. As time passes, more accurate information will become available.

If the police, mayor's office, governor's office or other authority issues an order, you ought to follow it. Instructions may direct evacuation near chemical spills at industrial plants or train derailments, power plant accidents, damaged dams, etc. If you are told to evacuate, do so

promptly and don't come back until an all-clear announcement has been given.

Directions regarding shelters, collection points for the
injured, sources of drinking water, and other information
will be broadcast when these plans are put into operation.

PLANNING FOR SELF-RELIANCE

If the earthquake causes widespread injury and destruction, emergency assistance will come from other cities
and states. The United States has a history of prompt and
generous support for disaster victims, at least in the short
run, and I have no doubt that within one, two, or three
days after a large quake, help will be available for almost
all victims. The American people have always pulled
together to help one another during and after a disaster.
Most people will be generous and helpful in sharing supplies, shelter, and assistance during the immediate crisis.

If, after the earthquake, you find yourself, alone or with
others, isolated by closed streets and lack of utility services, you may need to be self-reliant for a few days,
though. In most instances, it won't take long to get emergency help, but, if destruction is widespread, it might.
If you are away from home, or your building is unsafe
to re-enter, make plans for shelter.

Shelter.

The popularity of campers and recreational vehicles is
a positive factor in post-earthquake needs. Campers and
RV's are earthquake-prepared by their very design. If they
can handle the bumps and sways of highway travel, they
will withstand quite a bit of ground shaking. Unless a
garage has collapsed on it, a road-ready camper or RV
should be a great place for shelter after an earthquake.
Cars and other vehicles can also provide shelter. Just be
sure that they are parked where nothing can fall on them.
Tents and camping gear can also be used for shelter.

The danger of frostbite and cold exposure (hypothermia) is greater when you are tired, and a frightening experience can drain your energy. Wearing warm or protective clothing and keeping dry should be primary concerns. Try not to over-exert yourself.

Sanitation.

Don't flush the toilet until you are sure that you won't need the water in the tank and that the sewer lines are not damaged. Check accessible pipes for leaks and listen to the radio for public health warnings. If the lines are intact, and there is a swimming pool nearby, you can pour buckets of pool water in the toilet tank to flush it. Plastic bags to line a toilet, bucket, or other container may be used as a portable toilet. Use your stored water and soap for hand-washing and other cleaning needs. Wash your hands frequently and wear work gloves for protection.

Food and Water.

Check your supplies of water and food. Open closets and cupboards carefully in case things have fallen off shelves and are leaning against the doors.

Bottled water, melted ice cubes, water in the water heater, toilet tanks, and the liquids in canned fruits and vegetables, as well as whatever liquids may be left in the refrigerator, are possible sources of water. Be sure that you and the people for whom you are responsible drink adequate amounts of water.

If necessary, strain liquids through a clean cloth to remove bits of broken glass, but, if you have enough liquids, it is best to discard any that might be contaminated by glass or anything else. Water may be purified by boiling for five to ten minutes; or by adding ten drops of household bleach to a gallon of water, stirring, and waiting for thirty minutes; or with commercial purification products, following package instructions.

To use your water heater as a source of drinking water, take these steps:

1. Turn off gas or electric supply.
2. Close the water intake valve.
3. Turn on one or more hot water faucets nearby to allow air to enter the lines.
4. Use the valve at the bottom of the heater to collect drinking water with a hose or bucket. If the water appears rusty, let it run until the water is clear. *

If the electricity is off, use the foods from the refrigerator before eating the food in the freezer. Keep the freezer closed until you need its contents—the insulation and residual coldness will keep frozen food from spoiling for some time without electricity.

Don't use your fireplace for cooking or heat unless you are absolutely sure that the firebox and chimney haven't been damaged. Cook outdoors, using a barbecue, camp stove, or campfire in a safe, well-ventilated area. Share food and cooking energy with the people around you. A small charcoal fire can cook meals for several families. Don't bring a barbecue indoors, even if it appears to have stopped smoking because the smoldering coals can burn up your oxygen and poison you with carbon monoxide.

The San Fernando earthquake struck at six in the morning. By eight o'clock, neighbors were already cooperating on an outdoor neighborhood breakfast. People shared bacon, eggs and coffee prepared on a camp stove on the sidewalk. Another family connected their freezer to a gasoline-powered generator and offered to share freezer space with neighbors whose frozen goods would eventually spoil without electricity. The most striking feature of this community spirit was that most of these people barely knew one another before the shared experience of terror brought them together. But by a month or so later, most had returned to their original relationships, which consisted of a wave as they drove by.

Figure 7-3. Trained Red Cross volunteers often assist with damage assessment, as this man is doing after the 1987 Whittier Narrows earthquake. (Photo courtesy American Red Cross.)

Figure 7-4. This modern building collapsed into the street during the huge Mexico City quake of September 1985. (Josh Lichterman photo.)

Cleaning Up.

Once critical needs have been met and arrangements for shelter, food, and water have been settled, you can begin the job of cleaning up. This will also be the time to take a second look at the damage and watch for any problems you may have overlooked. If telephone receivers have fallen off the hook, replace them.

If it hasn't already fallen, examine the chimney for structural damage. Carefully check it and the fireplace, noting any cracked bricks or mortar, and looking for a new separation where the fireplace and chimney join the adjacent walls, ceilings, and roof, both indoors and out. During the earthquake, the chimney, with its great weight, may have moved at a different rate than the rest of the structure, resulting in a slight separation where they connect. If this separation is quite pronounced, or if there are wide or continued cracks (through adjacent bricks) or a tilt in the chimney, you should consult the local building safety inspector. Until you are assured of its safety, stay out of the building because of the danger of aftershocks that might cause further damage or topple a weakened chimney.

Check the building thoroughly, indoors and out, looking for cracks, sags, and other irregularities. After an earthquake, stucco buildings often have a crack where the walls join the foundation—another result of different masses moving at different rates. This hairline crack in the stucco around the base of the building is probably not a symptom of serious structural damage. Look for cracks or sagging in the ceiling, walls, and floors. Check the connections of built-in cupboards and other units to the walls and ceilings. Continue to be alert for the smell of leaking gas. Check your water heater and other appliances. Remember that aftershocks may cause further damage. If you have doubts about the structural integrity of a building, stay out of it until a professional inspector can be consulted. Report structural damage to your local Department of Building and Safety, which will conduct an inspection.

Cleaning up after the earthquake is bound to be difficult, especially without electricity and running water. You don't have to clean up the whole mess right away. Sit down and take a look at it first. Take some pictures. Store some memories. When you clean up and repair the damage caused by an earthquake, keep a complete record of everything that was broken or damaged. You may need this list for filing an insurance claim as well as for claiming a loss on your income tax returns. For valuable items, it would be best to save the pieces to corroborate your claims. Special costs, which you may have incurred as a direct result of the earthquake, should also be recorded and receipts retained.

Beginning Your Emotional Recovery.

The period after a damaging earthquake could be a difficult one. People's nerves are on edge, and each aftershock aggravates the tension. We will need to be patient and gentle with one another. Recovering from what seems like a life-threatening experience will take some time. Sorrow and concern over deaths, injury, and damage contrast with relief and joy over our own survival. The seemingly capricious nature of an earthquake, causing no damage here and great damage there, is difficult for us to handle.

Individuals react to this kind of stress in many different ways. Some people need to talk about it at length, describing their experiences and reactions and observations over and over again. Others feel a longing for peace and quiet and solitude, in direct contrast to those who need to touch and hold onto their loved ones.

The period of recovery will go on for weeks, months, or even years, depending on the impact of the experience. The inevitable earthquakes to follow will have a tendency to set back recovery, at least temporarily.

Sleep difficulties are very common following earthquakes. Having trouble falling asleep, nightmares, and waking in the middle of the night are normal reactions.

Sudden noises or vibrations such as a helicopter overhead or a big truck passing will recall our earthquake impressions, and we may find ourselves very "jumpy" and easily startled. If sleep difficulties or other emotional upsets continue for a few weeks or more, and particularly if they are interfering with our lives, a mental health professional should be consulted.

As we take care of the jobs that must be done following an earthquake, we should be sure to take care of ourselves, too. We should make sure that we're getting enough rest, wearing comfortable clothing, and eating and drinking as regularly as possible. We will need to be patient with ourselves and others. Everyone who goes through the earthquake will have some reaction, and these reactions will vary widely. Living through a damaging earthquake can be one of the most unique experiences of our lives, and our emotional reaction to it will blend into the rich tapestry of its memory.

8

Special Concerns:
Babies and Children

The Parent or Caregiver.

When you are caring for a child, you will want to protect him or her especially if you aren't together when an earthquake strikes. If you happen to be in another room, at the other end of the building, or even outside, you will be tempted to run to the child. This is a very powerful urge, but try to resist it. Your child will need you after the earthquake, and if you are injured, you may not be able to take care of the child afterwards. *The important thing for you to do during the earthquake is to protect yourself.* This won't be easy, but running to be with your child could endanger your life. So take cover in the closest safe place, hold on, and, if possible, call to the child with directions and reassurance.

If you are with your child at the time of the earthquake, take cover together in a safe place as described in Chapter 6. Once you're in the safe place, stay there. One mother in the Whittier Narrows earthquake braced herself in a doorway of her home while holding her baby. A frightened neighbor screamed and pounded on their door, and the mother moved toward the door. The ground was still shaking, and a bookcase tipped over on mother and baby when they moved away from safety. The injuries were minor, but they could have been serious.

151

When the ground stops shaking, proceed carefully. Check on the child or children and assess the situation in the building as you check them for injuries. If an evacuation is necessary, move carefully, and take essential equipment with you. Expect aftershocks. Plan ahead, moving from safe place to safe place within the building. Go outside only while the ground is still. Be confident and reassuring. Everything will be all right, because you've planned ahead and know what to do. If you are caring for older children, listen and respond to their concerns. If there are neighbors or others nearby, enlist their help so that the building can be inspected for fires and potential fires. Follow the procedures outlined in Chapter 7.

Infants and Toddlers.

In one respect, it's easier to care for a baby in an earthquake than an older child. Earthquakes aren't particularly frightening to infants. They're used to being carried here and there, lifted up, jostled—often without warning. Loud noises startle babies, of course, but the sounds of an earthquake aren't any worse than any other loud noise. The baby's experience is so limited that an earthquake doesn't seem extraordinary. So long as baby's caregiver is calm (or pretends to be) and reassuring, the baby won't be emotionally upset.

Bumper pads in the crib or bassinette and soft sides on the playpen will protect the baby while the ground is shaking. Select sturdy, stable baby equipment with low centers of gravity. Be sure that there is nothing that can fall on the baby such as tall furniture, hanging plants, mobiles, light fixtures, pictures, or mirrors. Chapter 5 details how to secure these furnishings.

In child-proofing your home, be particularly careful about earthquake hazards. The crawling baby or child on a kitchen floor might be hit by objects falling from cupboards during an earthquake, so be sure to install strong latches on all cupboards, not just the ones within baby's reach.

Baby Supplies.

The equipment and supplies listed in Chapter 4 will cover many of your baby's needs, but some special attention is appropriate. The baby grows so fast that checking supplies annually is not enough. If you've stored newborn-sized disposable diapers in January, they'll be too small in September. When baby begins eating solid foods, the menu changes monthly.

The basic principle is to store at least three days' worth of everything that your baby will need. This includes:

> formula
> bottles or nursers
> baby food
> juice
> disposable diapers
> baby wipes
> diaper rash ointment
> prescribed or recommended medications

Add a diaper bag to the earthquake kit in your car so that you'll always have at least one day's worth of baby supplies. Keep formula, food, teething rings, pacifiers, changes of clothing, blankets, diapers, and plastic bags for diaper disposal.

Always keep your regular diaper bag ready to go. When you return home after an outing, repack the diaper bag with fresh diapers, clothing, and other essentials.

The Child's Bedroom.

Children's bedrooms should be readied just like an adult bedroom, with accessible flashlight, eyeglasses, and shoes. The beds should be away from windows and sliding glass doors, and out from under heavy things which might fall. Shatter-resistant plastic film on the windows will protect children from shattering glass. I don't use bunkbeds for my children—I'm afraid that someone would fall off, or that the upper one would fall, or that the whole unit could tip over. If you decide to use them, be sure that the bunks are very sturdy, cross-braced, and securely anchored to the wall studs.

Preschool Children.

Beginning around age two, a child can be taught some safety principles for earthquakes. The "drop" or "duck and cover" drills taught in school can be introduced in low-key ways. Repetition and practice will help the child learn.

Begin by talking about earthquakes in your own words, explaining:

> Earthquakes are part of nature. They make our mountains by moving a tiny bit at a time. The earth is so big that when it moves only a little bit, the ground shakes hard. Everything on the ground shakes too. Ask your child, "What shakes?" The child can name things with you: Houses. Trees. Rocks. Fences. Toys. Walls. People. (The list can go on and on.) "Earthquakes can be scarey, like thunder and lightning, but we know what to do. We get under cover. Where do you get under cover in this room? Show me. Good! Now keep holding on as long as the ground is shaking!"

You can make the drill into a game, calling "Earthquake! Duck and cover!" with the child showing you safe places. Praise all the right answers, and correct the wrong answers by showing better alternatives. Keep the tone positive, never describing or threatening what might happen by choosing the wrong place. The correct response to an earthquake is to take cover in the closest safe place, and we want our children to learn to do this automatically. Be generous with praise for quick and smart choices. Repeat the game daily at first, then weekly, and then about every other week. If you have pets, read Chapter 10, and be sure to teach your children not to touch the pets during or right after an earthquake.

If your child goes to pre-school, talk to the teacher about the earthquake plans there. Be sure that your planning complements the school's. Try to use the same words and phrases used by the school; if the school says, "Duck and cover," or "drop," then you should do the same at home.

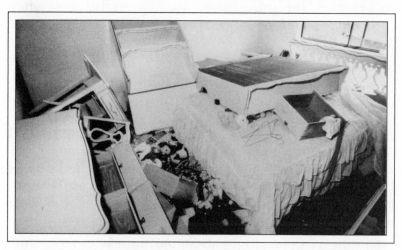

Figure 8-1. Tall furniture in this girl's room fell onto her bed during the Morgan Hill, California, earthquake. Fortunately, she was not at home when the earthquake struck. (Photo courtesy Bill Gates.)

Figure 8-2. The desks in this Mexico City classroom are holding up the floors of the collapsed school. Dropping under these desks would have saved children's lives. (Josh Lichterman photo.)

Always have a signed emergency card with up-to-date information at the school. Decide who will pick up the child at school in the event of an earthquake. This plan must be consistent and simple, not depending on telephones. If the designated person is other than a parent or guardian, this information must be on the emergency card at school in advance.

School-Aged Children.

All schools in earthquake-prone areas should have earthquake drills, just like the air raid or bomb drills we used to have when I was in school. Children are trained to drop under their desks or tables, and hold on, whenever the teacher shouts the command, "Earthquake! Duck, cover, and hold!" This preparation can be reinforced at home when families practice together and locate the safest places.

Children can be taught about earthquakes in the same way that they learn about other processes of nature and other safety rules. Describe earthquakes in words and concepts appropriate to the child's age. When my children were under ten, this is what I told them:

> When an earthquake happens, the ground and everything on it shake for a little while and then the shaking stops. Trees, people, houses, all the things inside houses ... everything shakes. After a while, the ground might start shaking again, and then it will stop again.

> There are earthquakes every day, but most are too small to feel. Once in a while, a little larger earthquake will jiggle things, and, every now and then, the ground shakes hard enough to make things fall down. Sometimes people get scared. Sometimes, but not very often, people get hurt by an earthquake, and, when they do, it's almost always because something has fallen down on them.

That's why, in school earthquake drills, the teacher says to get under the table. If something, like a piece of the ceiling or a light bulb, falls down, it will hit the table and not the person. The teacher tells you to hide your eyes because sometimes windows or light bulbs break and the little pieces of broken glass could bounce around and might get into someone's eye.

In our house, the safest place is in the hall-way or under the big table. But if you're in bed when you feel an earthquake, just stay there until it stops. Then, when the ground is still, we'll all meet in the hallway. If you're outside, sit down where you are until the ground stops shaking. Then come to the front sidewalk, sit down, and wait for the rest of us.

What you tell your children will depend on your own situation, and the maturity level of each child. Discuss with your older children what to do if you are not with them when an earthquake strikes. In emergency situations, school officials usually keep the children at school until the parents pick them up. Check with the principal of your child's school regarding its emergency procedures.

The up-to-date emergency card at school is important for all ages. If you have designated someone to pick up the children after an earthquake, tell the children about the plans. If you intend to pick them up yourself, let them know, and explain that it might take a while to get there:

If there's an earthquake or some other big problem while you're at school, I will come to get you. I know that school is a safe place for you. The teachers will take care of you until I can get there. They will keep all the children in a safe place, probably outside on the playground until everyone has been picked up.

If some kids have been picked up already, you might begin to wonder why it's taking me so long to get there. Remember that I work in a safe

place, and I know what to do. But if the streets
are blocked, I might have to walk, and it might
take a long time for me to get there. It makes
me feel good to know that you will be taken care
of until I come.

Talking over these plans lets the child know how
important it is for him or her to stay at school. Sometimes,
in the confusion following an earthquake, teenagers have
simply left their schools to go home or to check on a
younger sibling. You can support the school's plan by
explaining the need for your son or daughter's cooperation. Most children are more willing to do something
when they understand the reasons behind it. You want
your child to stay at school after an earthquake, because
the environment outside the school might be dangerous.

Teenagers.

I learned firsthand how important it is to be clear about
your expectations during an emergency. A few hours after
the Whittier Narrows earthquake, my sixteen-year-old
daughter and some of her friends left their high school,
dropped by our house, where they left a note, and went
on to a friend's house to go swimming. Fortunately, an
adult was there, and they had left notes, but they could
have found themselves in a situation they couldn't handle.
I hadn't explained the risks to her, and because we were
so well prepared, the earthquake hadn't really seemed
like a big deal to her. She and her friends had a wonder-
ful day.

If the students are already at school, it is better that they
stay there at least until the normal close of school. If the
environment is potentially unsafe, which means if there
is quite a bit of damage in the area of the school or where
the students live, they should be kept at school until
parents come to pick them up.

In a damaged area, there are many risks. For example,
there could be an explosion from leaking gas as a person
walks along the sidewalk. An aftershock could damage

buildings, injuring the student on the way home. In the 1983 Borah Peak, Idaho, earthquake, two children were killed by debris from the partial collapse of a concrete block storefront, which fell on the sidewalk. There could be dangers at home, too. If no one is at home, and the door is opened, the draft caused by the opening door could move a cloud of leaking gas to a pilot light, causing an explosion.

The Schools.

Schools are doing a better job of getting prepared, although there's a long way to go. One way of making sure that your school's plans are effective is by enlisting the support of the PTA or PTSA to work with school administrators. The Federal Emergency Management Agency now offers an Earthquake Safety Program for schools to assist with information and training.

Schools should have a written plan, regular drills, a hazard reduction program, staff training in first aid, rescue, and fire suppression, and disaster supplies. Some schools ask each student to bring a small earthquake kit to school. Typically, the child brings a zip-lock plastic bag with a few single-serving cans or packages of food such as juice, crackers, tuna, and fruit, plastic utensils, adhesive bandages, an emergency blanket or large plastic trash bag for warmth and rain protection, and sometimes, for younger children, a note from the parent (an all-purpose "I'm thinking about you" message). The PTA at many schools has supplied each teacher with a classroom emergency kit containing work gloves, first-aid and sanitation supplies, and other items that could help meet immediate needs.

The Child Alone at Home.

When your child reaches the age where he or she is left alone at home, even for a very short period, be sure that your instructions are clear. Be very specific about how to handle emergencies and where to get help. The child should know what gas smells like and be warned to go get help if gas is leaking, but until age sixteen or so, it's not a good idea to ask the child to turn off the gas at the meter. In the first place, it's hard to turn it off. Secondly, a younger child might decide to practice, and that would be dangerous. Tell your child to go outside and get help if gas is leaking.

Let your child know which neighbors are most likely to help. There should be more than one person to depend on, because one might be injured or unavailable. Tell your child to leave a note letting you know where he or she has gone. Have a regular message system and a place to leave notes for one another.

The Babysitter.

Sometimes the babysitter is a child too, and it's not reasonable to ask more of someone else's child than you would your own. The young babysitter can't be expected to assume full responsibility for all your possessions. Taking cover during the shaking, evacuating everyone afterwards, and trying to get help for fires, leaking gas, or injuries is a reasonable expectation. Let the babysitter know where the evacuation area is, where the emergency supplies (especially flashlights and first-aid kit) are kept, and how to get help. Remind the sitter that his or her safety and that of the children is the most important concern.

The adult babysitter should be made a full partner in earthquake preparation, understanding what to do and where supplies are located.

THE CHILD'S EMOTIONS

Most of us are upset after an earthquake. We react in different ways, but it takes some time before our emotions recover. We adults usually recognize when we need some quiet time or when we need to talk. Emotional recovery is new to children and they need our help, patience, and understanding.

Stay Together.

Children need to be with their parents or other secure adult when they are fearful. Keep the child with you if at all possible, and don't leave a child alone after an earthquake. This is a simple and important part of caring for a frightened child, and it often meets the adult needs too. We need to be with the ones we love when we are upset, frightened, or worried. Hugging, holding hands, sitting and talking together makes us feel better.

Carry on with the jobs that need to be done following the earthquake, but keep your child with you, unless it would not be safe. If there are two parents, one can stay with the children while the other inspects for damage, cleans up, and does the necessary work. Sometimes parents feel guilty about having to leave the child; this period will be tough enough without adding guilt to it. If you must leave the child, find the best care possible, and remember that you are doing the best you can in a difficult situation.

Talk About It.

Encourage children to talk about their feelings. Answer their questions truthfully, but reassuringly. Playing "earthquake" seems to be a healthy way for children to work through their emotional responses to these uncontrollable events. Children will often follow the examples set by adults; if parents and teachers take on a confident and upbeat attitude, children will too. Unfortunately, the reverse is true too. If adults are fearful and anxious, children will follow the example.

Be open and honest with your child. Explain what has happened and what it means for you. Be honest about feelings, too. Listen to your child and observe his play to discover what specific fears he might have. Sometimes these fears are unrealistic, and the parent can reassure the child. For example, if the child is worried about the house sliding down the hill, the parent can show him how the house is attached to the ground.

If, on the other hand, the fears are reasonable, parents can still be reassuring. If the child says she is worried that an earthquake will wake her up at night, the parent might respond that he thinks about that sometimes too. They can make plans together about what they will do if an earthquake does wake them up. Then they can talk about what they plan to do in the morning, and gradually move on to talking about more positive things.

As time passes, you may overcome your own anxiety sooner than the child, and it can become irritating to have a child "glued" to your side. Patience at this point will pay off. The child will regain independence when he or she is ready, and it will probably be sooner if you aren't

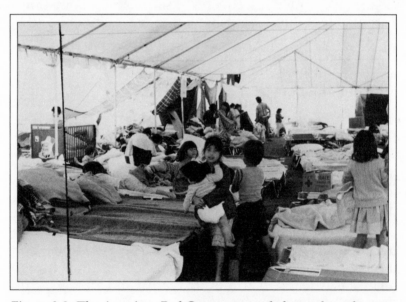

Figure 8-3. The American Red Cross sets up shelters where there are large numbers of homeless people. This tent was set up after the 1987 Whittier Narrows earthquake. Children adapted well and played happily here. (Photo courtesy American Red Cross.)

contributing to the anxiety by pressuring or insisting. Try to get the family back on its regular schedule, but don't expect everything to be normal.

Regression.

It's normal and expected for children to regress a little bit when they're upset. For a period of days or weeks, you will need to be patient about bedtime difficulties, thumbsucking, regression in toilet training, and similar challenges.

Problems at bedtime or sleeping are very common after an earthquake. The child may want to sleep in the adults' room or bed, or may not want to go to bed at all. For a few days or even longer, while the whole family is pretty upset anyway, it's fine to be flexible, so long as you are comfortable with the arrangements.

Often a nightlight, bedtime story, and a little extra attention will help a child go to sleep in his own bed. If the child seems so upset that he cannot sleep in a room alone, his mattress on the floor of the parents' room might be a temporary solution. But explain at the outset that this is just for a day or two, until things get back to normal. Accept and acknowledge the child's fears, while being confident that he will be back in his own room by Tuesday (or whatever day you choose). These bedtime anxieties occasionally appear a few weeks after an earthquake, and the same understanding and patience is needed.

Sometimes it takes a child (or adult) quite a while to recover from this kind of emotional experience. Remember that aftershocks will be occurring and may set back emotional recovery for adults and children. If, after a few weeks, you don't see forward progress in your child's recovery, it is probably time to call in a professional. Mental health professionals or clinics help many people re-adjust after an earthquake.

Look for the Positive Side.

A large earthquake and its aftermath can be a great adventure. As much as possible, find the positive in this experience. Take pictures and encourage the children to draw pictures. Make a scrapbook of newspaper clippings. Use the earthquake experience as a learning tool. Read and research together about what causes earthquakes and how they are measured. See who can guess the Richter magnitude of each aftershock. This will be a period in your lives that you will always remember. Even very young children retain memories of particularly vivid experiences. You and your children are sharing this experience and creating memories to last forever.

9

Special Concerns: Disabled and Elderly People

The basic principles outlined in this book apply to everyone, but there are some situations that require special attention. Earthquake preparation for people with disabilities and elderly people is really for all of us. We all hope to grow older eventually, and an earthquake could leave any of us disabled by an injury or even the loss of eyeglasses or contact lenses. Many of us will be in the position of trying to help people with disabilities after the earthquake, and we need to know how best to help.

I am including concerns for both disabled and elderly people in this chapter because their needs are often similar. Of course, people with disabilities are of all ages, and both this chapter and the preceding one will apply to children with disabilities. Older people have some advantages in an earthquake. Their experience and wisdom often prevents them from panicking, and their slower, more deliberate movements are appropriate for earthquake safety. People with disabilities often have these attributes as well, regardless of age.

Eliminate Hazards.

If you cannot take cover, you must be certain that there is nothing that could fall on you. This is particularly important for wherever you spend a great deal of time, such as your bed, desk, work station, and chair. Besides the possibility of injury, fallen debris could make it impossible for you to walk or to move a wheelchair, making evacuation impossible.

During the 1983 Coalinga, California earthquake, a paralyzed young man watched helplessly as his special telephone fell to the floor, out of reach. Other household objects also fell, and his wheelchair would not move, so he could not go to a safer area. After the earthquake, friends came to check on him and were able to help him.

Special equipment such as telephones and life support systems should be securely fastened down with Velcro or some other means. Tanks of gas such as oxygen should be belted in place with two chains bolted to the studs of the wall. If tanks of gas are knocked over with damage to the valves, they can propel themselves around the room like missiles.

Stock Additional Supplies.

In addition to the supplies listed in Chapter 4, stock those supplies which are essential to your safety and comfort. Maintain at least a week's supply at all times. If you rely on life support systems, be sure to have a good emergency energy back-up system. Wear a bracelet or necklace giving essential medical information. If it would be difficult for you to turn off your gas, have an automatic shutoff installed.

Additional supplies to keep at your bedside, at work, and with your wheelchair include:

> police whistle or loud bell
> flashlight
> "Go" Kit:
> > extra medications, supplies, and equipment (such as bladder pads, catheters and cleansing solution)
> > hearing aid batteries
> > pencils and paper
> > patch kit for wheel chair tires
> > copies of prescriptions

list of essential medications and dosage
written description of current medical condition
relative's name, address, and telephone number
doctor's name, address, and telephone number
food for guide dog
contact lens solution

Planning at Work.

When you rely on elevators to get into your workplace, emergency evacuation can be a real challenge. There should be two accessible emergency exits, and a realistic evacuation plan. Take part in the disaster response preparations at work, and make sure that the plans consider people with disabilities. Communication for people with visual or hearing disabilities should also be addressed.

There are devices such as 'evacuation chairs,' traction devices that go downstairs like army tanks, as well as emergency chutes for evacuating the disabled. If your company is relying on these devices, make sure that their use is practiced regularly.

The Buddy System.

There should be at least two buddies assigned to you at work, and you should try to find two or three more at home. These buddies are willing to check on you after any emergency or disaster, and to assist you when needed. Most people are happy to help, but they need to know what to do.

First, explain to them that you're getting prepared for an earthquake or other disaster, and urge them to do the same. Tell them about your special needs and concerns. Familiarize them with any equipment you use. For example, show them how your wheelchair works, whether the arms come off, how to patch the tires, and go up or down a curb. Let them know of any particular harms that untrained help might cause; if taking you out of your wheelchair might hurt you, show them the correct procedures. Tell them about your essential supplies and where they are kept. Invite the neighbor buddies into your home to let them become familiar with the layout and the location of supplies. Give a spare key to a trusted neighbor.

Sometimes the buddy system is reciprocal; two people agree to check on one another. In condominiums, apartments, and in Neighborhood Watch groups, this system works very well. Other times, it can only work one way, but the assisting buddy will be rewarded by the satisfaction of being there to help someone.

During the Earthquake.

We advise people to take cover because the greatest danger is from falling objects. But it is important that after you take cover, you will be able to move to a safer place if necessary. If it would be impossible or even difficult for you to get out from under a desk or table, don't get under it.

If you are in a wheelchair, stay in it. Turn away from windows. Move the chair into a doorway with your back toward the hinge, or move away from hazards such as falling books or furniture. Set the brake on the chair and, if possible, lean over or hold a pillow, book, or even an empty wastebasket over your head and neck for protection.

If you have difficulty moving, but are not in a wheelchair, assess the situation. Often, you will be safest just staying where you are. *If you are in bed or sitting down, stay there while the ground is shaking.* If you are on your feet, sit down on the floor or in a chair if it is very close. Several older people in the 1983 Coalinga, California earthquake received fractures when they were thrown to the floor while trying to get to a doorway.

The Caregiver.

Just as a parent feels like running to a child when an earthquake strikes, you will want to protect the person you are caring for, even if you aren't together when an earthquake strikes, and you may feel like running to the person. The important thing for you to do at this time is to protect yourself. This won't be easy, but you will be needed after the earthquake, and running could endanger your life. So take cover in the closest safe place, hold on, and if possible, call to the other person with reassurance.

When the ground stops shaking, proceed carefully. Check on those for whom you are responsible, and assess the situation in the building as you check them for injuries. If an evacuation is necessary, move carefully, and take essential equipment with you.

After the Earthquake.

What you do after the earthquake depends on where you are and what your personal situation is. Follow the guidelines in Chapter 7. Check yourself carefully for injuries. Use the telephone only if you desperately need help. If you are trapped, use your whistle, bell, or flashlight to attract attention. Pound or bang on windows, walls, or pipes, or wave a sheet or jacket out the window.

To Evacuate or Not?

The decision to evacuate is an important one. If evacuation is easy, and if there is any possibility of fire or structural damage, then by all means, evacuate to a safe outdoor place. If evacuation would be difficult, then take your time in deciding. In general, the rule is to evacuate if there is a threat of injury by remaining where you are. If there is no fire, no gas leak or chemical spill, and no significant structural damage, then you do not need to evacuate, particularly if the evacuation might be hazardous to you.

If it is clear that everyone must evacuate, the people with disabilities should be evacuated last. This is for your protection, so that you will not be injured in a rush of people. If you are in a wheelchair, on crutches, or use a walker, be sure to ask for assistance. It takes at least two people to assist a person in a wheelchair. Give directions for helping you calmly and clearly. Tell people what items you will need at the evacuation area.

Helpers, Buddies, and Rescue Workers.

First, try to locate everyone who might need assistance. Look for people with visual or hearing disabilities. Be respectful and considerate. Try to help without endangering human dignity. Get enough people to do what is necessary without injuring anyone.

When assisting someone with a disability, begin by asking the person, "Do you need help? How can I help you?" Listen to the answer. If you have trouble understanding, ask them to clarify or write down the requests. The person who has a disability is in the best position to know the type of assistance required. The person who rushes to help without asking first could cause serious injury. For example, the standard "fireman's carry" could be fatal to some people with respiratory problems.

When assisting someone who uses crutches, a walker, or canes, remember that these will be needed in the evacuation area. Also, the person with disabilities will need supplies and a coat or other protection from weather.

Evacuate the disabled people last, and remember that a hazardous evacuation is the last resort. It requires at least two people to take a person in a wheelchair up or down a flight of stairs, and it is dangerous. If there is no compelling threat to safety, a person in a wheelchair would be better off remaining in the building.

In the evacuation area, again ask those with disabilities how you can help. Their needs will be similar to the rest of ours: personal care, someone to talk to, and information on the current situation.

10

Protecting Your Pets

As we plan for human safety and for the protection of the things that belong to us, we should remember the other important members of our household: our pets.

SAFETY WITH PETS

Earthquakes are very frightening to us, but household pets can be so upset by the ground shaking that they revert to their more primitive ancestral behavior. The safest course of action is not to touch any animal while the ground is shaking. Make this a family rule, and be sure that your children understand.

Most animals will instinctively protect themselves, and if you attempt to interfere with them, they may turn on you. The sweetest dog or cat who sleeps at the foot of your bed every night might scratch or bite you out of fear and panic, especially if she feels that she's being restrained while she wants to escape.

It's best to let dogs and cats do what they want to do during the earthquake. They may blame you for causing the upheaval, or they may come to you for security. One of my friends told me that during the 1987 Whittier Narrows earthquake, she, her husband, and daughter stood in the doorway as their two dogs barked and crowded between them for protection.

171

Cats.

Normal cat behavior during earthquakes seems to be to run away and hide, whether indoors or outdoors. Do not interfere with this behavior. Often, indoor cats will hide in a closet or under a bed for a few days after an earthquake, while the upset owner goes to great lengths to coax the cat to emerge. The typical individualistic cat will come out when he's ready, and nothing you can do will change his mind, although I suspect that ignoring him might speed up the process a bit.

Outdoor cats frequently disappear for a few days after an earthquake. They probably do just what the indoor cats do—find a safe place and hide out for a while. Our cats have always come back after every earthquake, but on rare occasions, a cat will disappear for good. After a few days, you might begin regular checks with the local humane society to try to find the lost cat. Don't give up hope too soon. It's not unusual for a cat to disappear for a week or two before returning home.

One veterinarian noted that the most frequent injury to cats after earthquakes is infected claws. Apparently, when the earthquake strikes, a panicky cat will use its claws to start running, and if the cat happens to be on a sidewalk or street, the claws get injured. The owner usually doesn't notice that the cat has been hurt until a week or so later, when the paws have a discharge or odor that the owner notices. It would be a good idea to check your cat's claws from time to time after an earthquake.

Dogs.

While the ground shakes, some dogs run and others hide. Still others want to be near their owners. It's not unusual to hear of dogs being lost after an earthquake. I think that if they are unrestrained outdoors or can jump a fence to escape during an earthquake, some dogs begin running out of fear and don't stop until they are exhausted. By then, they may have lost their way. It's quite

Figure 10-1. Curiosity brought this cat out of hiding soon after the 1987 Whittier Narrows earthquake. (Photo courtesy American Red Cross.)

common, a few weeks after a damaging earthquake, to hear of packs of dogs causing trouble. Once these frightened, hungry animals join together, they revert to more primitive behavior.

Of course, the best strategy is to prevent this by keeping dogs in a fenced yard, but sometimes the fences are damaged by the earthquake, or the dog darts outside when a door is opened. My friends in Altadena, quite a distance from the Whittier Narrows earthquake, lost their beloved Labrador Retriever when they opened the front door after the big aftershock. The dog slipped out and they couldn't catch her.

Be sure that your dog and cat wear identification tags all the time. Many people have had their pets tattooed for identification as well. If your pet is lost after an earthquake, keep checking the local shelters, put up posters, and place advertisements in the "lost and found" section of your newspaper.

Other Pets.

Birds, snakes, hamsters, and other caged animals can be kept safe from earthquakes by making sure that their cages won't fall or open when the ground shakes. Hanging cages should be hung in such a way that the cage can't jump off the hook. Stands should be attached to the wall. Adhesive Velcro® strips are good for securing cages to a shelf. Plastic cages are safer than glass in case of breakage.

Aquariums are difficult to secure, because they are heavy and usually made of glass, but securing the aquarium stand to the wall, and using some kind of a fence to prevent the aquarium from sliding off usually will protect it. Because of the aquarium's great weight, it is very important than it never be kept where it might fall on a person or block an exit.

Animal Predictions.

Can animals predict earthquakes? There are many stories of restless horses the night before the 1906 San

Francisco earthquake, and many people report dogs barking or running around just before earthquakes. It is true that some animals behave in unusual ways just before an earthquake, but most seem to be taken by as much surprise as we are. This unusual animal behavior is so difficult to measure that it hasn't been very helpful in predicting earthquakes, except in China, where reports of unusual behavior are filed along with observations of well water levels and other geologic phenomena.

Scientists have not agreed about why some animals become restless, nervous, or unwilling to be indoors or fenced in just before an earthquake. It may be that animals are closer to the ground than we are, or have four feet so that they may be more sensitive to tiny foreshocks. Another possibility is that animals are more sensitive to the changes in the magnetic field and other geologic changes, which precede large earthquakes.

Chinese seismologists used to rely on a wide variety of indicators to help them formulate earthquake predictions, but, in the past few years, the Chinese have backed away from the use of animal behavior as a predictor.

United States scientists have conducted a number of studies to evaluate the theory that unusual animal behavior precedes earthquakes. For example, one theory was that the number of reports of lost dogs, cats, and birds increased just before earthquakes. A three-year study found no correlation. Pocket mice were observed in a simulated outdoor habitat, and some differences in behavior were observed before a swarm of earthquakes, but it could not be proven that the earthquakes (and not the weather or some other factor) caused the behavioral changes.

Most seismologists have abandoned the idea of attempting to identify unusual animal behavior as a precursor to an earthquake. The difficulties in waiting for earthquakes, evaluating and measuring the behavior, and repeating the experiment for verification seem overwhelming at this time. But the stories of unusual animal behavior before earthquakes have been told since ancient

Greece in the year 373 B.C., and they will undoubtedly continue.

Preparing Your Home.

Take the same precautions to make your home safe for pets as for people. But be especially sure that nothing can fall on the place where your pet normally sleeps, and be sure to install latches on cupboards and anchor heavy furniture so that nothing will fall on your pet.

Always keep at least a week's supply of food on hand because emergency assistance may be available only for people at first. If you have a large pet, be sure to store additional drinking water too. Ask a neighbor to care for your pets if you are not at home when an earthquake strikes.

After the Earthquake.

Your pet may need extra patience and reassurance after the earthquake. The animal may be jumpy, irritable, or noisy—just like the rest of us. Add some extra security by keeping the pet inside, if possible. A little special attention with petting and grooming might be reassuring, but don't force the issue. Like people, some animals just don't want to be touched when they're upset. If you notice some behavioral changes, be patient and careful.

Planning for your pets' safety is an important facet of responsible pet ownership. Keep them in mind as you get ready for an earthquake.

Part IV

Earthquake Prediction and Future Planning

11

The Science of Prediction

December 3, 1990 will be remembered by many Midwesterners for what didn't happen: a huge earthquake didn't jolt the New Madrid fault—or any other fault, either. Iben Browning, a New Mexico scientist, had predicted that strong earth tides created by the alignment of the sun and moon could act as a trigger for a large fault which seems to be ready to release its stored energy in an earthquake. Browning gave the New Madrid fault a 50-50 chance for creating a M7.0 earthquake in the first five days of December.

Although most seismologists discounted the "prediction" and the theory behind it, the news media gave it tremendous coverage, which created enormous public interest, some bizarre reactions, and even some responsible preparedness activities. Civic leaders seemed to take the prediction very seriously. Schools were closed, kits and other supplies were sold, and emergency drills were conducted. Many people simply left the area and others camped outdoors despite the bitterly cold weather. Reporters and camera crews moved in to be ready for the event—or non-event, as it happened.

The New Madrid Fault didn't move on December 3rd, but the prediction left a lasting impact. Midwesterners are finally recognizing that their area is due for a damaging earthquake sometime within the next thirty years. It might not be a repeat of the greater than Magnitude 8.0

179

earthquakes of the 1811-1812 winter, but even a moderate earthquake in the Mississippi Valley could cause tremendous damage and tragic numbers of dead and injured people. Area geology permits strong ground shaking to be felt over a huge area. Damage will probably total billions of dollars because of the huge number of unreinforced brick and stone buildings. Due in part to Browning's prediction, the legislatures of the several states in the New Madrid area are beginning to consider adding seismic safety requirements to building codes and retrofitting old buildings, particularly schools.

Do we really want to know?

One of the scariest aspects of an earthquake is that there's no warning that it's coming. We know when a hurricane is on its way, and we can learn to recognize when conditions are right for a tornado or lightning storm, but earthquakes just happen. They would not be quite so frightening if there was a bit of warning first. People have been trying to predict earthquakes—or, at least, identify some warning signs that a earthquake is about to happen—for thousands of years, but progress is just beginning.

The science of earthquake prediction is still in its infancy. There have been successes and failures, but there is reason to be optimistic that at least some earthquakes could be predicted. We are in a transition period now, and a system for preparing and responding to earthquake predictions is beginning to be implemented.

Won't a prediction cause fear and panic?

Surprisingly, most people react fairly rationally when they learn than an earthquake has been predicted in their area. First, many are suspicious and doubt the reliability of the prediction. In the New Madrid case, most people who looked for more information about the prediction found out that it wasn't very reliable. A lot of people will refuse to believe even a scientifically valid prediction. Many tap into the four stages of denial:

- It won't happen.
- If it does happen, it won't happen here.
- If it does happen here, it won't be that bad.
- If it does happen and it is that bad, there's nothing that I can do about it anyway!

Instead of trying to overcome widespread fear, disaster planners believe that the hardest job will be to get people to overcome denial and take the prediction seriously. Fortunately, most people also react by seeking more information, and the news media and public agencies will respond to fill that need.

This was certainly true in the New Madrid area. Every newspaper, television and radio news program seemed to make some reference to the prediction, the fault, or earthquakes in general. Since the whole concept of earthquake risk was relatively new to the area, there wasn't a system to deliver clear, consistent preparedness messages to the public.

The American Red Cross, the Central United States Earthquake Consortium, and other reliable agencies found their advice diluted by poorly informed commentators. An expert interviewed on television might explain and demonstrate the "Duck, Cover, and Hold" procedure and then be followed by an interview with a person on the street who was convinced that the earth was going to open up and swallow him. As Browning's predicted date drew near, anxiety levels were undoubtedly raised by the inconsistent information, misinformation, and media "circus" atmosphere.

In 1991, when an official prediction was placed in effect in the Parkfield, California area, residents were advised of the risk of an earthquake and what they can do to protect themselves. There was no widespread fear and panic. Most people reacted by taking some steps toward preparedness. Studies indicate that, while they did the easiest and least expensive things, at least the reactions were positive.

PREDICTION FACTORS AND DEFINITIONS

Before we examine the state of the science and how we fit into it, we need to understand what a prediction is and who makes it. From time to time, there are news reports of earthquake predictions with little substantive information to enable us to evaluate them. Seismologists, as well as psychics, have been making earthquake predictions for years.

A statement that the San Andreas or New Madrid Fault is "due" for an earthquake is, after all, a prediction of sorts, even though it doesn't specify size or time. Generally, scientists now require that in order to be classified as a "prediction," the statement must include all four of the following elements: location, time, size, and a strong probability of occurring. And each of the elements must be fairly specific. The location must give the precise coordinates in latitude and longitude within one degree of error. The magnitude must be within a half step on the Richter Scale. The time must be fairly specific. Predictions are now classified as long term, intermediate term, and short term. An earthquake "forecast," on the other hand, doesn't specify time, only that an earthquake of a specified magnitude in a specified location will occur at some time in the future.

A newly developed system enables scientists to report their findings to a designated federal committee of scientists, the National Earthquake Prediction Evaluation Council (NEPEC), which reports to the United States Geological Survey (USGS). NEPEC advises the director of the USGS, who decides on the validity of a prediction and notifies the Federal Emergency Management Agency (FEMA), which issues the prediction and informs the governors of all states involved. The governors can then issue an earthquake "warning," which will be a directive to take defensive action to prevent the likelihood of injuries and damage. The warning will be public and the news media will also be informed. California is the only state with its own Earthquake Prediction Evaluation Council.

Advisories

When scientists advise that there is an increased risk of an earthquake in a certain area for a short period of time—usually three to five days—an advisory may be issued by an Office of Emergency Services. Typically, advisories are issued following earthquakes which might be followed by other earthquakes. Many moderate strike slip earthquakes (in which the movement along the fault is horizontal) are preceded by foreshocks, smaller earthquakes which occur within three days and ten kilometers of the larger earthquakes. When a earthquake occurs along a strike slip fault, seismologists consider the possibility that it is a foreshock to a larger earthquake. If there is such a chance, they may recommend that an advisory be issued.

Psychics.

In the past, various psychic persons, seers, or fortune tellers outside the scientific community have predicted that an earthquake would strike a certain area on a certain date, but their success rate has been insignificant, at best. I haven't seen any evidence to convince me that anyone yet has tuned into the energy aura that may surround the crust of the earth—or whatever it may be necessary to tune into—to the extent of being able to reliably forecast seismic activity. That is not to say that such sensitivity is not possible, but it does not appear to be available to us at this point. And, if it is available to some persons, I don't know how we would distinguish in advance between the true psychic and the charlatan. When I use the term, "prediction," in this chapter, therefore, I refer to statements made by qualified scientists using methods generally approved by the scientific community.

Precursors.

Predictions are based on the idea that particular events sometimes occur before some earthquakes, and that if these events could be observed and interpreted correctly, they would indicate that an earthquake is going to occur.

These events, which appear before earthquakes—but do not cause them—are called "precursors." They may consist of one or a combination of irregularities, or even the absence of certain phenomena, such as a lack of seismic activity in a region under strain.

Paleoseismology.

Another key factor in predictions is the written or geologic history of earthquakes. The faults themselves can indicate the size and history of earthquakes, and radiocarbon dating is used to date decomposed organic material preserved underground. Newspaper records, old letters, Indian folk history, and even tree rings have been examined to determine the dates and magnitude of past earthquakes.

Some geologists examine faults in order to discover the length of intervals between earthquakes to determine when a fault might be expected to move. Another important element in developing predictions is the study of patterns of seismicity. Locating epicenters, sizes, and dates of earthquakes over time enables scientists to detect patterns, recurring sequences, and gaps.

Recent scientific studies have revealed that—three hundred years ago—a huge earthquake struck the coastlines of Northern California, Oregon, and Washington. Researchers have found the remains of huge trees which were killed by salt water, and they have heard an Indian legend of the prairie being swallowed by the ocean. This great earthquake, which would have registered M7.5-8.4, suddenly dropped a section of the coastline below sea level.

The Pacific Northwest coastline is known as the Cascadia subduction zone, where the smaller Gorda plate is pushing under the huge North American plate. For years, scientists have recognized that this process has fueled a chain of volcanoes and occasional moderate earthquakes.

But now it appears that the plates are locked and are building up strain, which will be released in another huge earthquake, possibly as large as M9.5. The new research has led many seismologists to consider this the most dangerous fault in the United States, posing a grave risk in the Pacific Northwest.

THE CHINESE PREDICTION EXPERIMENTS

Scientists and historians have been observing and recording earthquakes and their effects for about as long as they've been recording anything at all. The Chinese are unequalled in this field. Whereas written accounts of earthquakes in the United States go back only two or three hundred years, depending on when settlements were established, Chinese records date back as far as three thousand years.

Recently, Chinese historians have compiled all the recorded information available about earthquakes into one comprehensive catalogue of earthquake activity in China. One of the most surprising facts revealed by this catalogue is the irregularity of some earthquake patterns. For example, the 1920 earthquake in Kansu Province, which killed 180,000 people, occurred in an area that was earthquake-free for 280 years before 1920. And the worst natural disaster in history, the 1556 Shaanxi earthquake, which claimed 830,000 lives, followed a thirteen-year period of low earthquake activity.

It is no surprise then that China should have taken an early lead in earthquake prediction and warning. The large number of stone houses, poor construction, and overcrowded conditions have contributed to high casualty rates in earthquakes there. They were confident that, with enough information, earthquakes could be predicted, and they were willing to undergo the inconvenience of evacuating their homes in the chance of avoiding the devastating human death toll recorded in past earthquakes.

The Chinese political and economic system allowed trial and error in developing an earthquake warning system without the tremendous economic and legal entanglements that complicate the system of prediction and warning in the United States. Disturbed by the news of many deaths caused by a series of three earthquakes in March of 1966, China's Premier, Zhou Enlai, responded by ordering Chinese scientists to develop an earthquake prediction system. Since then, the earthquake catalogue was compiled, and four-hundred ground deformation observatories were established and equipped with instruments to detect earthquake precursors. The Chinese do not yet have a fully computerized system for storing and interpreting data from the various stations, nor have they spent as much time on theoretical studies as western scientists; however, their mandate to predict earthquakes and issue warnings, combined with broad public support of their work, enabled them to issue several accurate predictions. Seismologists in China analyzed data from historic records, instrument readings, and large numbers of observations reported by scientists, farmers, and other workers. There was widespread attention to unusual animal behavior and changes in the water level of wells as precursors of earthquakes. During the 1970's and early 1980's, the whole country was used as an earthquake prediction laboratory, and scientists received more criticism for *not* issuing a warning than for warning of an earthquake that did not occur.

China's greatest success in earthquake prediction was the M7.3 earthquake of February 4, 1975 in the city of Haicheng, in northeastern China. The decision to keep a close seismic watch on the area was made in 1970 on the basis of a pattern of small earthquakes with epicenters that seemed to be moving toward Liaoning Province, where Haicheng is located.

The local seismic observatory noted changes in the earth's magnetic field, and a rise and tilt of the earth's surface during 1973 and 1974. Other precursors were noted in 1974: an increase in the number of small earthquakes, well water becoming muddy, an increase in radon gas in wells. By early 1975, reports from zoo-keepers and farmers indicated unusual animal behavior: listless tigers, fish jumping from rivers, pigs refusing to enter their sties.

On February 1, the number of unusual reports began to escalate. Well water levels rose suddenly; hot springs stopped flowing; frogs were observed jumping through holes in the ice; animals refused to enter their folds; and a series of earthquakes was noted in a previously quiet area. Scientists met, compared notes, and reported to civil authorities. At 2:00 pm, the warning was issued:

> There probably will be a strong earthquake tonight. We require all to leave their homes, and animals to leave the fold, also, to move the weak and old. There will be four movies shown outdoors at the city square tonight.

Despite bitterly cold weather, the people cooperated. Patients were moved from hospitals. Families, vehicles and farm animals were moved out of buildings. Five-and-a-half hours later, the large earthquake began. It caused widespread damage, collapsing up to ninety percent of the structures in some areas. There were very few injuries among the three million people who lived in the area, because they had left their buildings and moved into open areas.

Since the successful prediction of Haicheng in 1975, Chinese scientists have had successes and failures as they attempted to effect a reliable earthquake prediction system. They have observed that certain precursors occur years before an earthquake, while others are observed months, days, or hours before a shock. By categorizing observations within time frames, scientists attempted to "read" the pattern of events leading up to an earthquake. When precursors, which typically occur a few weeks or a month or two before an earthquake were observed, the people were mobilized to keep watch for other changes.

This mobilization had the effect of alerting the population to the possibility of an earthquake, while enlisting large numbers of observers looking for unusual animal behavior and other anomalies. During this time, emergency preparations were made, including setting up large light-weight bamboo shelters for people in case they would be asked to leave their homes. When the number of precursors increased sharply with observation of a variety of different indicators, and geologic and historic investigations indicated that the area was vulnerable to a strong earthquake, scientists notified civil authorities, who would issue a warning.

Seventeen months after the successful prediction of Haicheng, a strong earthquake (M7.9) virtually destroyed the industrial city of Tangshan on July 28, 1976. Fifteen hours later, a strong aftershock (M7.1) compounded the disaster, as did three other M6.0 or larger aftershocks the same day. Chinese authorities have reported that the death toll at Tangshan was 243,000, and with roughly twice that number of injuries. But it could have been much higher. The city had been built over a maze of coal mines, and many sections of the city collapsed into huge pits. Although some precursors had been noted by scientists, and the area was being watched closely, no warning had been issued.

In hindsight, one anomaly that may have been very important was recorded on a gravimeter, a device which measures gravity and changes in the gravitational pull. It gives an indication of change in the elevation of the surface of the earth or in the density of the rock below the device. The largest change ever recorded on a gravimeter was recorded in Tangshan shortly before the earthquake. At the time, the significance of this information was not appreciated.

Some observers have suggested that a political power struggle existing at the time may have prevented the issuance of a warning, but Chinese scientists argued that there were not as many different types of precursors evident in Tangshan as there were before Haicheng. There were no foreshocks, and they had not completed geologic studies of the area prior to the earthquake. The Tangshan fault had been considered to be a minor one.

Clearly, some earthquakes have far fewer precursors than others, and these will be much more difficult to predict. Surprisingly, earthquake prediction is now considered unreliable in China and the project has been reduced in scope. Russia and Japan have recently emerged as important forces in the science of prediction.

JAPANESE PROGRESS IN PREDICTIONS

Located on the "Ring of Fire," Japan is one of the most earthquake-prone countries in the world. Like China, it has a long recorded history that includes details of past earthquakes. Seismological studies began in Japan a hundred years ago, and some early scientists were pioneers in the study of earthquakes.

The Japanese have now taken the lead in earthquake prediction and warning, with a national network of instrumentation coordinated by the Japan Meteorological Agency. The JMA collects data on crustal movements, such as uplifts and tilts, earthquake activity, changes in geomagnetism and electric resistivity, and changes in the level, temperature, and gas concentrations in ground water.

So far, one single precursor has not emerged as the key to predicting earthquakes everywhere, but Japanese scientists have observed that seismic activity and changes in the concentration of gases in underground water can be very good indicators.

The Japanese earthquake prediction program began in 1965 as a national project, working within five-year programs. In 1978, the Large-Scale Earthquake Countermeasures Act was passed with the goal of predicting the expected major earthquake in the Tokai region, south of Tokyo, where large earthquakes have occurred in the past, but not for many years, and where crustal strain appears to be accumulating. Japanese scientists are gathering data in hopes of predicting the earthquake in order to minimize the disaster. The law would require the prime minister to issue a public warning and requires public and private organizations to respond to the warning. A concerted program for education and preparedness is underway. There is great concern in Japan about the seriousness of the coming earthquake. The Tokyo municipal government has estimated that this earthquake might claim 30,000 lives, and some consider this estimate to be too conservative.

Japan has had some success in predicting earthquakes and greater success in identifying precursory activity after an earthquake. Researchers at Tokyo Institute of Technology have predicted, with a probability of greater than ninety percent, a M6.5 or greater earthquake to occur off northeast Japan before 1998. They do not expect severe damage, because the epicenter of the earthquake will be offshore.

EARTHQUAKE PREDICTION
IN THE UNITED STATES

The seismologists of the world are cooperating in the search for a reliable system of earthquake prediction, and American scientists are making great contributions to the field. There are not as many moderate and larger earthquakes in the United States as there are in China and Japan, so there are not as many opportunities for prediction.

Some of the investigatory work in earthquake prediction takes place in the laboratory through the study of theoretical models, while field researchers locate, study, and evaluate faults at their sites. Instruments are utilized to measure changes in the distance between geographic points, changes in the tilt of the land or the magnetism of rocks, uplifts or "bulges" and downdrops of large areas of land, underground methane and other natural gas pressure changes, variations in levels of water and gasses in wells, changes in the gravitational pull and the electrical resistivity of rocks, and changes in the speed in which sound waves travel through rock. All of these are seen as possible indicators of a build-up of geologic strain. They may indicate that stress is increasing to the point where movement along a fault will be triggered.

Seismic Gaps.

Soviet scientist, S.A. Fedotov, observed a pattern of Japanese earthquakes along a known fault. By locating twelve large earthquakes along the fault and plotting the location of aftershocks for each earthquake, he noticed that each area lined up next to another without overlapping. He also noticed some areas where there had been no major earthquakes since 1904 or earlier. These areas were described as seismic gaps. Over the next few years, four large earthquakes struck, three of them in the areas Fedotov had indicated were overdue for a earthquake. In 1968, two American scientists identified a gap near Sitka, Alaska, and forecast a earthquake in the area. In 1972, a large (M7.6) earthquake occurred in the forecast region.

There are two kinds of seismic gaps; the first is the unruptured area along a fault zone or seismic belt. The second is a period of abnormally low earthquake activity (seismic quiescence) in a specific area, which is later struck by a moderate or larger earthquake. This second kind of seismic gap has been observed all over the world as a precursor. When this seismic gap is surrounded by a circle or doughnut pattern of increased earthquake activity, the phenomenon is known as a Mogi doughnut, named after Kiyoo Mogi of Tokyo University. A Mogi doughnut appeared in the five years before the 1983 M6.8 Coalinga, California earthquake.

Squeaky Doors.

Recent observations of a recurring sequence of earthquakes along the West Coast of North America have revealed some interesting data, which may assist in earthquake prediction. The pattern formed by the earthquake in Imperial Valley, California in October 1979, the Mammoth Lakes, California series of May 1980, and Baja, California about a week later, repeated a similar sequence in those areas during 1940, 1915, and possibly, 1857. The order of events in a pattern of this sort varies, but the associations have been repeated.

Volcanic eruptions may also fit into these recurring patterns. For example, Mexican or Cascade volcanoes have erupted close to the time of major southern California earthquakes. The involvement of volcanoes in earthquake patterns demonstrates their common origin beneath the earth's crust. One explanation for recurring sequences of earthquakes may be that movement along plate boundaries might cause weaker areas to break loose sooner, followed by movement along progressively stronger sections of the plate. These earthquakes may occur in sequences that repeat at intervals. One scientist refers to this as the "squeaky door" model of seismic episodes: when something in the mantle disturbs the crust, it always creaks in the same places.

Planets, Tides, and Weather.

Some scientists are investigating the controversial theory that tides, eclipses, and planetary alignments may exert unusual gravitational stresses on the earth, which may affect seismic activity. Browning's prediction for the New Madrid fault was based on this theory. The moon and the sun do cause tides in the solid crust of the earth as they do in the oceans, but the tides are not as large. The theory is that these tides could add to or detract from stress on faults, and could act as a trigger for some earthquakes that are just about to happen. Scientists at Caltech and elsewhere downplay this theory, seeing very little or no statistical correlation.

There is no such thing as earthquake weather. Rain, snow, wind, high humidity or low, mild or severe weather make no difference. Earthquakes strike in all kinds of weather and at all times of the day and night. When enough stress builds up, the earth moves.

The Parkfield Prediction.

The only approved earthquake prediction in the United States at this time is for a moderate (approximately M6.0) earthquake to occur at Parkfield, California, about mid-way between San Francisco and Los Angeles. The earthquake is predicted to occur before 1993, with a ninety-five percent probability. This intermediate term prediction has been approved by both the National Earthquake Prediction Evaluation Council of the U.S. Geological Survey and the California Earthquake Prediction Evaluation Council. The San Andreas fault zone in the area of Parkfield historically has generated a moderate earthquake about every twenty-two years, and the last one was in 1966.

Parkfield presents an opportunity for geologists and seismologists from around the world to have their instruments in place to gather data before, during, and after the earthquake. If possible, they hope to record and evaluate precursors, and perhaps, issue a short term prediction with a time frame of somewhere between fifteen minutes and several days, during which the earthquake would be expected to strike.

Whether a short term prediction is issued or not, the instruments will record the earthquake. Laboratory experiments cannot replace actual studies of ground shaking and measurements of the effects of ground shaking on buildings and other structures. Studies have been made to determine the geology in the Parkfield area to interpret the effect of the underlying geology on the earthquake waves. Instruments are in place to record strong motion, acceleration forces, liquefaction, ground vibrations, and the performance of bridges, schools and pipelines. After the Loma Prieta earthquake, instruments which measure electro-magnetic radio waves were installed in the Parkfield area in hopes of duplicating the unusually high readings which were recorded a few hours before the earthquake.

The prediction did not cause widespread panic or even deep concern among the residents. Earthquakes were not new to them, and the moderate size of the predicted earthquake didn't appear to bother them. Parkfield is a small town, surrounded by farmlands and vacant land.

Damage and injury should be minor. In every sense, this prediction appears to be beneficial. The residents have been cautioned to take precautions, and the network of monitoring instruments is in place. If and when there are strong indications that the earthquake is about to happen, a short term prediction will be issued, and the residents of six neighboring counties warned.

The Parkfield prediction offers possibilities for gaining information that could ultimately save thousands of lives. The data collected may help to predict an earthquake elsewhere on the San Andreas Fault and on faults all over the world.

Regrettably, the commitment of the United States government to saving lives through the prediction of earthquakes can be questioned. Federal funding cutbacks have reduced, rather than expanded, the monitoring of phenomena such as the levels of radon gas in well water. Whether the Parkfield Prediction is a success or failure, the goal of saving lives and property should be enough to justify federal funding to maintain a network of seismic monitoring and investigation in all earthquake-prone areas of the United States.

EMERGING AND CHANGING THEORIES

Comparing notes with Japanese and Soviet scientists as well as close study of recent earthquakes has led United States seismologists to rethink some of their previous assumptions. The relationship between the length of time during which precursors are observed and the size of the eventual earthquake is not fully understood. It was previously thought that the longer the time frame, the larger the earthquake, but this is now in question.

The relationship between the location of precursors and that of the eventual earthquake is being questioned, too. It was thought that precursors occur in the same general area of the earthquake, and that the geographical range over which precursors were observed might indicate the size of the expected earthquake. However, before the 1979

(M6.6) Imperial Valley, California earthquake, sharp increases in radon gas levels were noted in wells two hundred miles away. After the earthquake, the levels dropped to normal. The observation of precursors at such great distances would have indicated a much larger earthquake, according to previously accepted theory. Now it appears that the underlying forces that cause earthquakes also cause other events, which can be observed over a much wider area.

It was also assumed that all major earthquakes had precursors, even though they might not be observed, but most scientists now think that some major earthquakes occur with very few or no precursors. On August 6, 1979, near Hollister, California, an (M5.7) earthquake took place at Coyote Lake. The Hollister area experiences many earthquakes and almost continual "creep" along the Calaveras Fault and is, therefore, very well instrumented. The only anomalies observed before the Coyote Lake earthquake, however, were a very slight increase of radon gas and a very minor tilt. Both phenomena had been observed previously at these low levels without being followed by an earthquake.

As is often the case with scientific study, the more that is discovered about precursors of earthquakes, the more complex the processes appear to be. What seems to hold true for one area may not work in another, and every so often an earthquake appears to break the "rules." Several earthquakes have been accurately predicted, however, and the learning continues. Each new piece of information adds to the growing body of evidence upon which a system for making predictions can be based. In the interim, scientists are not keeping their discoveries a secret. Their work has been and will be revealed to the public through scientific articles and news reports. When possible indicators cause professional concern, the public will be informed.

The science of prediction is still developing, so it is likely that damaging earthquakes will continue to strike without warning. We must keep working on reducing the risks to people and property by stabilizing or demolishing hazardous buildings, developing better land-use practices, and improving government, business, and individual preparedness.

Clearly, the possibility exists now for a short term earthquake prediction to be issued in any area known to be seismically active. The National Earthquake Prediction Evaluation Council will evaluate the data presented and issue the warning if the earthquake appears to be likely. Official agencies and the general public will be urged to take protective measures. The next chapter will describe what can be done when an earthquake is expected.

12

When An Earthquake
Is Expected

The time may come when you will expect an earthquake. This chapter will examine the reasons for expecting one, the purpose of notifying people when to expect an earthquake, and the possible responses by individuals and public officials.

WHEN WOULD YOU EXPECT AN EARTHQUAKE?

The Short Term Prediction.

When a short term prediction is issued by the Earthquake Prediction Evaluation Council, the state office of Emergency Services will be notified, and the news media will also be informed. The state agency will notify concerned county agencies and their response will depend on the likelihood and the potential impact of the earthquake. If loss of life and widespread damage is expected, the response may be the declaring of a state of emergency, mobilization of emergency personnel, and other actions. For a less serious prediction, the response will be considerably less.

After An Earthquake.

Moderate and larger earthquakes are followed by aftershocks, which are earthquakes. Typically the aftershocks are progressively smaller and further apart, but it is not at all unusual to experience good-sized aftershocks a few minutes, hours, days, and even weeks afterwards. The weeks and months after experiencing an earthquake are a time in which more earthquakes might be expected.

The Foreshock.

About five percent of southern California's earthquakes turn out to be foreshocks, and the statistics for other areas are probably roughly the same. An earthquake that is followed within five days by a larger earthquake at or near the same location is considered to be a foreshock. Roughly a comparable percentage of earthquakes are followed within a year or two by another earthquake of similar size in the same general vicinity, exclusive of the aftershocks. The statistics may vary in other areas, and the odds are obviously small, but it is logical to consider any moderate or damaging earthquake to be a low level earthquake alert.

SEVERAL SECONDS WARNING.

An earthquake warning system is a possibility now. Because radio waves travel faster than earthquake waves, it is possible to be warned of a coming earthquake a few seconds or even a minute or two before it strikes where you are. The interval between the warning and the earthquake would depend on your distance from the earthquake and the device that sensed it.

Bullet Trains.

Japan Railways has an earthquake warning system for its bullet trains, and it has been operating for the past twenty years. Since the bullet trains travel at speeds up to one-hundred and fifty miles per hour, the risks created by an earthquake are very great, and when the 1965 (M6.0) Shizuoka earthquake damaged the six-month-old bullet train's tracks, the danger was clear. The first warning system, for the Tokaido line, was implemented the following year. There are now three bullet train lines, and each has a slightly different warning system.

The Tokaido line features twenty-five seismic stations, each about twelve miles apart. When the accelerometer senses a force greater than 0.04g of horizontal acceleration, the electrical power to the bullet train is shut off for about six miles on either side of the reporting station. When the power goes off, the train's brakes are automatically applied.

It will take about seventy seconds to bring a train from full speed to a complete stop, and the train will traverse about 1.4 miles during those seconds. The primary goal of the system is to prevent a train from crossing damaged track at high speed. The action is reported to the General Control Center in downtown Tokyo, which determines how long the trains should be stopped, how much track to inspect, and how to coordinate the trains on adjacent sections of track.

The Warning System appears to work well. In twenty years of operation, it has stopped trains about one-hundred times and the rails had been bent twice, but not so severely as to damage the train even at top speed. In the past seven years, there were four false alarms or shutdowns without an earthquake. Investigators have discovered and corrected the causes (a mouse, in one case).

Since the Japan Railways Warning System has not demonstrably saved lives yet, some people might consider it unsuccessful. The shutdowns have inconvenienced thousands of people, and the system is expensive. But the potential for saving lives is certainly present.

A California System.

An unplanned test of an early warning system was set up during the Nimitz Freeway rescue work following the 1989 Loma Prieta earthquake. When aftershocks were detected by the U.S. Geological Survey's sensors, radio warnings were automatically sent to the rescue site, allowing workers up to 27 seconds to move off the precarious freeway debris. This successful use of technology which permits the continuous monitoring of a seismic zone with automatic transmission of warning signals proved its worth.

The California Division of Mines and Geology studied the cost and potential benefit of an earthquake warning system in California and released a report in early 1989. The report failed to conclude that the benefits of such a system would be justified by its enormous cost. However, the National Research Council spent a year analyzing *real-time earthquake monitoring*, and recommended in 1991 that a completely automated prototype system be developed. To keep costs down, they noted that California's existing regional seismic networks could be upgraded into an early warning system.

Using the most up-to-date monitoring technology, a prototype warning system sounds like a science fiction writer's dream. Real-time information about a quake which is actually underway, but has yet to arrive at a given place might include the size, location, and duration of the quake *as it is happening*. It might be possible to direct elevators to the closest floor and open their doors when a warning system is activated. Sirens in schools could alert students and teachers to "drop" under their desks. Fire trucks and other emergency vehicles could be moved outdoors. An automatic response system at a manufacturing facility might include recorded safety warnings, assembly line and computer shutdowns, and gas or chemical shutoffs. The response might even be varied for different magnitudes and durations. This concept opens a new era in emergency response planning, conceivably saving many lives as well as preventing damage.

RISK FACTORS AND ALERTS

If you expect an earthquake soon, you should take special steps, beyond your normal earthquake preparation, to prevent damage and injury. These special steps might be categorized as "full alert" or "partial alert" status, and they are described in the Checklists in Appendix I.

Your response would depend on your own evaluation of what the risk might be to you. The factors outlined here should help you evaluate that risk. If one or more of these factors places you at high risk, you should respond with a full alert:

1. The predicted size of the anticipated earthquake.
2. How close you are to the expected epicenter.
3. How close you are to the fault that is expected to move.
4. The nature of the land beneath you. The most dangerous would be loosely compacted alluvial soils, human-placed "fill"—which is even more hazardous if it's water-saturated, unstable slopes, and low-lying coastal zones.
5. The earthquake vulnerability of the structure.
6. The credibility of the prediction.

In the western United States, a full alert response would be appropriate if, for example, you are within approximately twenty-five miles from the epicenter of an expected great earthquake, or if you are within about ten miles from a moderate one, even though your building and geology are stable. East of the Rockies, multiply those distances by ten or more. If your geology or building place you at risk, you should evacuate even at greater distances from a predicted quake. If you live or work in an unreinforced masonry building, you would be wise to evacuate before *any* expected earthquake.

The alert status should be maintained until after the earthquake and several aftershocks. Wait at least twenty-four hours if the warning was for a great earthquake, if an earthquake has already caused damage, or until you have been assured to your satisfaction that the warning was a false alarm. The problem with a predicted earthquake that fails to occur, unless it strikes a different area than expected, is that the indicators that led to the prediction will probably remain, and the possibility may exist that the earthquake will occur later than anticipated.

EVACUATION

Evacuation is one part of the full alert response, but it doesn't mean getting in your car and driving as far and as fast as you can. Obviously, there would be an incredible traffic jam and a host of other problems if even ten percent of a city attempted to do that. A more practical, realistic, and safer evacuation method in most cases would be to simply go to your nearby evacuation area. If you need to move further away from home or work, find a place out in the open such as a park, on flat solid ground. You might even wait in your car, if it's out in the open on level ground—and keep your seatbelt fastened.

People in some hazardous areas should evacuate to a greater distance, but still to the closest safe place. Unstable hillsides, those which have experienced problems in the past, for example, should be evacuated, as should land along faults and coastlines, and below dams, if a great earthquake is expected.

DISASTER MOBILIZATION STEPS

The reason that some concerned experts might be willing to risk public panic in order to press officials into action is that the government has in its power the means to save many lives as well as to take disaster mobilization steps, which would vastly increase available assistance. The following are measures that could be enacted if an earthquake were predicted to occur within a week or less:

1. Evacuate buildings previously identified as dangerous.
2. Evacuate low-lying coastal areas.
3. Mobilize emergency facilities—assembling additional staff, moving emergency vehicles out of garages, stocking emergency supplies, postponing elective surgery.
4. Lower the water levels in reservoirs.
5. Shut down nuclear reactors.
6. Shut down oil and gas pipelines.
7. Close vulnerable bridges, tunnels, and streets.
8. Secure toxic, incendiary, and explosive materials at industrial and research facilities.
9. Shut down dangerous manufacturing and construction procedures.

10. Close buildings of mass assembly such as theaters, auditoriums, and stadiums.
11. Broadcast advice on emergency procedures over radio and television.
12. Contact and advise segments of the population not reached by the news media, such as foreign tourists and non-English speaking residents.

If these procedures were to be implemented before a moderate or larger earthquake, loss of life would be reduced substantially, as would property damage. Any economic losses incurred as a result of these preparations would be more than justified.

As better systems are being developed for predicting earthquakes, local and state governments are working with federal representatives to build a legal framework for official response to a prediction. Striking a balance between the political, economic, and social repercussions of an earthquake advisory, which turns out to be a false alarm and the possible benefits of a warning issued before a strong earthquake is not likely to be a simple matter.

The goal is to issue an advisory that will save lives without causing panic or economic disaster. Some business analysts and public planners warn that a long-range prediction in a specific location could have serious economic effects. They envision a situation of panic with businesses relocating, reducing their inventories, postponing maintenance, and decreasing the workforce. Property values, according to this view, would plunge as people and businesses move out of the area, and recession, with all its attendant anxieties, might snowball. A short-term prediction of an earthquake, which doesn't occur, might have similar results. However in view of the dense population and economic activity of both Los Angeles and San Francisco, which have admitted the reality of the earthquake threat for years, this scenario seems unlikely to occur.

LONG-RANGE PLANNING

The official response to a prediction depends on the amount of time before the earthquake is expected to strike.

The steps previously outlined would be in response to a short-term prediction. Though not as dramatic, the steps which could be taken with a year or more of lead time could be equally significant in saving lives:

1. Identifying and vacating or reinforcing high-risk structures.
2. Improving land-use planning and management.
3. Upgrading the earthquake-resistance of key structures, such as bridges and dams.
4. Adoption and enforcement of stricter building codes.
5. Implementation of earthquake preparedness programs for the community.
6. Reviewing, rehearsing, and improving disaster response plans.
7. Development of post-earthquake redevelopment plans, including ways to avoid rebuilding on unstable land.

These are steps that any community should take even without a specific prediction, but the fact that in most areas they haven't been taken yet is discouraging. Progress is being made, especially with the problems of hazardous buildings and the elimination of dangerous parapets, but there is still much to be done. An official long-term prediction may give a push to unprepared communities.

At some point in the future, earthquakes *will* be predicted with some regularity, and civic authorities and individual citizens will have the opportunity to respond. We aren't at that point yet, but the United States is in the transition stage of preparing to respond to earthquake predictions. When a prediction has been made, we should hope that public officials take the appropriate steps to mobilize emergency facilities and reduce hazards. Whether they do or not, we as individuals can take steps to protect our lives and property. Since we can't depend on getting any warning of an earthquake yet, we ought to be making preparations as though a long-term prediction were in effect.

13

Learning From The Bay Area Quake

In June 1988, shortly after a M5.1 quake rolled through the Santa Cruz area, seismologists warned the public of the possibility that a larger earthquake might strike within five days. The reaction was calm and low-key. In fact, most people simply ignored the warning. But fire engines were moved outdoors, emergency radio equipment was checked, and critical emergency personnel were placed on call while they all waited for a bigger quake.

A year later, after a M5.2 quake on August 8, 1989 in the same area, a similar short-term advisory was issued. The United States Geological Survey had identified the Santa Cruz segment of the San Andreas Fault as having a high probability of causing a damaging earthquake within thirty years, and these moderate quakes could have been pre-shocks to a larger one. When five days passed without an earthquake, the advisories expired, and the area returned to its usual waiting stage.

Two months after the second warning, as Game 3 of the World Series was about to begin, a bigger earthquake rolled from Santa Cruz up into the San Francisco Bay Area. At M7.1, this was the earthquake anticipated by the seismologists. But it wasn't the "Big One," which could be a repeat of the 1906 San Francisco Earthquake in which the San Andreas Fault moved as much as twenty feet. Since 1906, energy has been building up along the San Andreas, and the October 17 quake released just a fraction of the strain which could break loose at any time.

It is not always a good feeling to be proven right, and, in this case, seismologists and disaster planners were just as horrified as the rest of the world at the death and destruction caused on October 17, 1989. It happened at 5:04 p.m., beginning eleven-and-a-half miles under the Santa Cruz Mountains along the San Andreas Fault, which, at that point, slants downward toward the southwest. The Pacific Plate moved about six feet northward and four-and-a-half feet upward. Seismologists call it the Loma Prieta Earthquake, named for the highest peak in the area. Some local people call it the "Pretty Big One."

The Medic Epicenter.

In Candlestick Park, ABC's World Series pre-game coverage was interrupted by the ground shaking. The announcer called out, "We're having an earth . . ." His words were cut short and the picture turned to static. Sports fans were the first in the outside world to know that a big quake had struck the area. The ground shook for only fifteen seconds, but that was sufficient to create a trail of terror, death, and destruction over a hundred mile path.

The quake had two epicenters—the real epicenter, where it began in the Santa Cruz Mountains, and the media epicenter in the Bay Area, where the world's attention was first focused. The damage was dramatic in the Bay area, and the camera crews which were on hand to cover the baseball game switched from sports coverage to the breaking news story that surrounded them.

One of the most horrifying scenes was the mile-long collapse of the double decker Cypress Street section of the Nimitz Freeway (Highway I-880) in Oakland. The columns which supported the upper deck failed, and the upper level collapsed onto the unfortunate motorists below. At first, it appeared that more than two hundred people could have been trapped or crushed in the mangled freeway. The death toll was, in reality, forty two, a mercifully small number considering the extent of the disaster and the time of day.

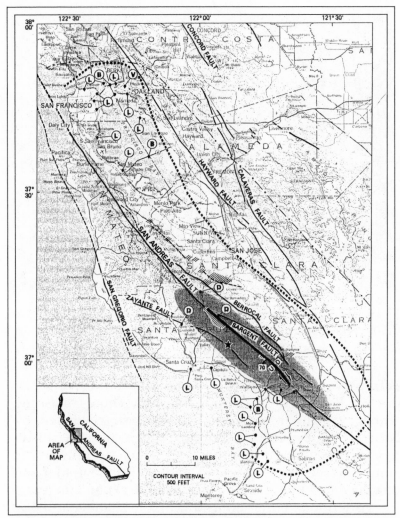

Figure 13-1. The Loma Prieta Earthquake. (Map courtesy United States Geological Survey.)

EXPLANATION

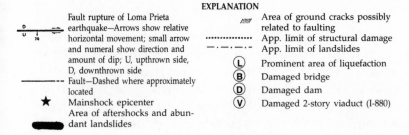

Fault rupture of Loma Prieta earthquake—Arrows show relative horizontal movement; small arrow and numeral show direction and amount of dip; U, upthrown side, D, downthrown side

Fault—Dashed where approximately located

★ Mainshock epicenter

Area of aftershocks and abundant landslides

///// Area of ground cracks possibly related to faulting

·············· App. limit of structural damage

—·—·—·— App. limit of landslides

Ⓛ Prominent area of liquefaction

Ⓑ Damaged bridge

Ⓓ Damaged dam

Ⓥ Damaged 2-story viaduct (I-880)

Figure 13-2. The Nimitz Freeway in Oakland collapsed due to the failure of the columns which supported the upper deck. (Photo courtesy United States Geological Survey.)

Transportation in the Bay Area was also disrupted at the San Francisco-Oakland Bay Bridge. There was some damage at the approaches to the bridge caused by liquefaction, but the most dramatic sight was the thirty-foot section of the upper roadway, which fell onto traffic lanes on the lower deck. The Bay Bridge had been designed to allow some flexing, but the expansion joints were extended to their limits during the shaking and one section simply pulled apart and fell.

Fire and Liquefaction.

The camera crews couldn't miss the plume of smoke rising from the Marina District shortly after the earthquake, so attention was turned to the residential neighborhood which was beginning to burn. The huge fire which consumed a third of a block was a secondary effect of the (literally) underlying culprit in the Marina District.

Figure 13-3. The third story of this building in the Marina District ended up at ground level. The first story was damaged by liquefaction and the second story collapsed. (Photo courtesy Florence G. O'Donovan.)

The main problem was the ground under the upscale homes and apartments. The area was once called "Washerwoman's Lagoon," and had been filled in to create land for the 1915 Panama-Pacific International Exhibition which celebrated both the completion of the Panama Canal and the full recovery of San Francisco from its devastating fire and earthquake in 1906. The buildings were cleared shortly after the exhibition, and the land lay vacant until the 1920s when the area was developed into a fashionable residential neighborhood. Ironically, the property which had been created to celebrate recovery from the 1906 earthquake actually created a far greater danger for the next big earthquake. Even more ironically, some of the landfill used was debris from the 1906 earthquake. The combination of old buildings (many with dry rot) on top of sandy soil with a high water table proved devastating on October 17th.

The Marina District's loose soil amplified the shaking and became liquefied as the ground shook, and the old buildings slid off their foundations or collapsed. The first floor garages of many buildings crumbled and were crushed by the collapsing upper stories. Pavement buckled, gas and water pipelines in the buildings and underground broke, and fires were ignited.

Without water to fight the fire, San Francisco was on the brink of another huge fire. But the city had a disaster plan, well-trained crews, and The Phoenix, a fireboat which had almost been cut from the city's budget the year before. Helpful volunteers came forward to carry the long firehoses, and the fireboat pumped water out of the bay to fight the fires. The lack of wind helped slow the spread of fire, and it was brought under control within a few hours. The emergency lasted several days, since an eight-block area had to be evacuated because of leaking gas and fears of explosions. Many people were not allowed to retrieve any of their belongings because their buildings were too dangerous to enter.

The Earthquake's Epicenter.

Meanwhile, cities and neighborhoods fifty miles to the south had also been severely shaken by the earthquake. The media's attention was concentrated on the Bay Area first, but Santa Cruz, Watsonville, Los Gatos, Hollister, and other areas closer to the Loma Prieta area actually experienced stronger shaking than did the Bay Area. Fortunately, the area closest to the epicenter is fairly rural and not densely populated. In the small cities nearby, many buildings collapsed and many more fell off their foundations. Landslides, buckled streets, and toppled chimneys were common throughout the area. Six people in Santa Cruz County and five in Santa Clara County were killed. Hundreds of people lost their homes.

Figure 13-4. Sand boils, such as these in the Marina District, are geologic evidence of liquefaction. Similar sand boils were observed in Oakland and Santa Cruz. (Photo courtesy United States Geological Survey.)

Figure 13-5. Strong ground shaking and liquefaction caused the collapse of this section of Highway 101 over Struve Slough near Watsonville. The support columns punctured the roadway as it fell. (Photo courtesy United States Geological Survey.)

Not Predicted, But Forecast.

Seismologists have been advising people along the San Andreas Fault that the segment in the Santa Cruz area was likely to have an earthquake greater than M6.5, so the Loma Prieta quake came as no surprise to those who had been listening. But the Bay Area had been lucky since 1906, when the last Big One hit, and most residents had never felt a major quake before. It was easy to ignore the threat. And, as bad as the Loma Prieta quake was for the Bay Area, a major earthquake with its epicenter nearby, instead of fifty-six miles to the south, will be far worse.

If earthquakes follow patterns, this could be the first step in an awesome trio. In October of 1865, a strong earthquake hit the same Santa Cruz area as the Loma Prieta Quake with very similar effects. Three years later, in October 1868, a strong earthquake shook the Hayward Fault close to Oakland, and, thirty-eight years later, San Francisco was devastated by the 1906 earthquake. Seismologists point out that with or without this pattern, there is still a strong likelihood of the "Big One" striking within the next thirty years, a mere moment in geologic time.

The Geologists and Engineers Were Right, Too.

Just as the earthquake came as no surprise to seismologists, its impact was not surprising to geologists and engineers. They knew which areas would be hit hardest and which structures were at the greatest risk. The California Department of Transportation (CalTrans) had been working on retrofitting bridges and highways, because early designs did not allow for the strong motion caused by quakes, and the Nimitz Freeway had been identified as a risk. The unreinforced masonry buildings were known to be hazards, especially when located on loose soils. Bay mud and landfill were known to increase the risk to structures, and the areas of greatest risk had been mapped, pinpointing the areas of the Nimitz, the Bay Bridge, and the Marina District. Landslides were expected in the Santa Cruz Mountains, and the earthquake triggered dozens of them.

It Could Have Been A Lot Worse.

As horrifying as those fifteen seconds in 1989 were, the disaster could have been much worse. The death toll of sixty-five was remarkably low. Every year, there are reports of more lives lost in a plane crash or a huge storm than the number of people killed in this earthquake. It is rather astonishing that the rush hour traffic was light and so few people were on the Nimitz Freeway at that precise moment. And if we focus on the deaths other than in the freeway collapse, the number was remarkably small. Many people were watching the baseball game, and would have been relatively safe in front of their television sets in their homes. The huge crowd in Candlestick Park behaved admirably, and that undoubtedly prevented injuries.

The fire damage could have been far worse, as noted earlier. The availability of the fireboat, the lack of wind, and the relatively small number of fires enabled the San Francisco Fire Department to handle the crisis, but it took all the available resources. It is almost incredible that, aside from gas leaks, there were no major hazardous material spills or leaks.

The main shaking only lasted fifteen or sixteen seconds, a short time for a M7.1 earthquake. Longer shaking would have caused much more damage. The small cities and countryside were hit hardest, while the densely populated San Francisco area, sixty miles to the north, escaped major shaking. Most of the Bay Area came through the earthquake extremely well. The damage there was almost exclusively in areas where the geology caused the seismic waves to amplify.

Most Of The Damage Was Preventable.

There is still somewhat of a random factor in earthquake damage, and some well-built buildings were severely damaged, but most of what happened to structures was expected. The cost-effectiveness of seismic reinforcing was clearly demonstrated in this earthquake. A few thousand dollars of structural improvements might have saved the Nimitz Freeway. Thousands of homes were lost for lack of investing a few hundred dollars each to anchor the home to the foundation.

One of the great tragedies of the Loma Prieta Quake was its effect on people's homes. Often, the buildings which fell off their foundations were completely destroyed, and most were not covered by insurance. As a result, not only did people lose their homes, but the loss often represented their life savings as well. Fifty percent of the homes in San Francisco may not be bolted to their foundations creating an enormous risk for the next earthquake.

The dangers of unreinforced concrete or brick buildings have been known since 1933, and yet too many of these buildings are still in use and have not been retrofitted. Combine the unsafe buildings with unstable geology, and it is no surprise when they collapse—except, perhaps to the people who live and work in them.

Thousands of people spent the morning after the quake cleaning up the things that broke when they crashed to the floor during the shaking. Most of this non-structural damage was also preventable, but people haven't bolted their furniture, put fences on shelves, latches on cupboards, and taken the steps described in this book to minimize damage.

Lessons For Personal Preparedness.

Earthquake preparedness experts focused their attention on the Loma Prieta survivors and victims to see if the advice we have been giving held up. It did. Taking cover in the closest safe place and holding on is still the best thing to do when you feel an earthquake. Trying to move across a room is too risky while the ground is shaking.

We know that sidewalks are dangerous places in an earthquake, and five people died in the Loma Prieta quake when a brick building collapsed on to the sidewalk. This earthquake was so short that those people probably didn't have a chance to take cover. But if you are in this situation, try to get inside the building while the ground is shaking. If you can't get into the building, then move away from the buildings.

After the quake, people needed prescription medication, flashlights, portable radios, and extra batteries for both—things that we have been telling them to have on hand. The next morning, people formed lines outside stores waiting to buy bottled water and the other supplies they would need to get through a period of time without their utilities.

The lack of electricity was a great inconvenience to those who were not prepared. Many people told of the frustration of waiting through the long dark night, suffering through the aftershocks, and feeling very alone because they didn't know what was going on. They didn't have portable radios, and many didn't think of turning on their car radios. Even with a radio, it was hard to get accurate information within the affected area.

The American Red Cross set up shelters for those who couldn't get home or whose homes were too badly damaged to enter. The help was welcomed, but many of these very independent people found it very difficult to accept the assistance. The shock of the tragedy was often mingled with feelings of embarrassment or guilt at not being prepared. Some people didn't even have a change of clothing with them, and this added to their discomfort.

Businesses experienced frustrating losses because of the loss of lifeline services. Two or three days without electricity, telephone service, and transportation translated into great losses even if the building or its contents had not been damaged by the earthquake. There were great differences between the businesses which had an effective disaster plan in place and those which had not done any realistic planning.

Getting Together Again.

One of the main areas where people were not prepared was in their reunification plans. The frustration of being separated from loved ones was enormous. The shutdown of some segments of the transportation system, and the disruption to telephone service meant that residents could not get home or make calls for some time, and the anxiety of not knowing how their relatives were made the experience much worse. Because of overloading, there was often a delay in getting a dial tone after the earthquake. Cellular phones worked fairly well, but as more and more people put these phones in their cars, the system will become more vulnerable to overloading. It is still best not to use any telephone after an earthquake unless you are calling to report a fire or medical emergency.

At Candlestick Park after the earthquake, television cameras showed the ballplayers walking out with their arms around their wives and children. They illustrated one of our basic human needs—to be able to touch the ones we love when there is a calamity. An earthquake makes us want to be with, to hug, and to talk to the people we care about. After a big earthquake, it may not be possible to get together with those we love for hours, or even days. And we won't even be able to talk to them on the telephone. It is an enormously frustrating experience, and the only thing that will make it a little easier is to have talked about it ahead of time. So make your plans, talk to your loved ones, and keep talking to your children regularly to let them know that after an earthquake, you will eventually all be together again, but it may take some time.

Loma Prieta's Lesson For The World.

The most important lesson that we have to learn is to get moving on reducing our earthquake hazards. On both the governmental and individual levels, we have to be willing to invest time and money into protecting ourselves from earthquake damage. When the seismologists advise us that there is a risk of an earthquake in a particular area, we have to listen, because these experts know what they are talking about. California probably leads the nation in preparedness, and yet it still has a long way to go. The other sections of the country with high earthquake risk must make the commitment now to reduce their seismic liabilities as quickly as possible. Being ready for an earthquake will save lives and property, but it has to be done before the earthquake.

Appendices

Appendix I

Checklists to be Earthquake Ready

STEPS TO TAKE FOR PREPAREDNESS

1. Identify the safest spots inside your home and workplace to move to when an earthquake starts.
2. Eliminate earthquake hazards in your home and workplace. Anchor tall furniture, belt water heater, install latches on cupboards, safety film on glass. Protect valuable equipment and possessions by bolting, belting, securing with Velcro® or silicon adhesive, or moving to safer storage.
3. Designate evacuation areas—meeting places, usually outdoors, for your home and place of work. Make a family plan for reuniting after an earthquake.
4. Assemble Earthquake Kits for home, work, and each car:
   Backpack or other container
   Flashlight with spare batteries
   Water (half-gallon per person)
   Food (day's supply of high energy, ready-to-eat food
   First aid kit (smaller kit in car)
     (bandages, soap, antibiotic ointment, antiseptic solution, chemical cold compress, table salt, acetaminophen or aspirin, anti-diarrhea medication, scissors, safety pins, tweezers, thermometer, tissues, matches, pocket knife, three-day supply of essential medication, spare eyeglasses, first-aid manual)
   Portable radio with spare batteries
   Plastic trash bags
   Local map
   Blanket or emergency blanket
   Sanitation supplies (plastic bags, tissues, premoistened towelettes, sanitary napkins)
   Heavy-duty work gloves

Walking shoes and socks (in kits for car and work)

Jacket, hat, comfortable clothes (in kits for car and and work)

Communication kit (stamped, addressed post cards, pen, phone numbers, coins)

Sleeping bag (optional)

Snow and cold weather protection (in cold climates)

5. Stock your other provisions:

Fire extinguishers

Extra flashlights (one at every bedside)

Power failure lights

Tools for turning off utilities

Other tools: crowbar, work gloves, shovel, duct tape, broom, dustpan, pen, paper, adhesive labels

Additional water (minimum three gallons per person

Additional food (minimum three-day supply) (pet food too)

Sanitation supplies

6. At your bedside, keep shoes, flashlight, work gloves, bathrobe or jump-in clothes, eyeglasses, essential medication if needed.

7. Identify and know how to avoid earthquake hazards in your community.

8. Consider the purchase of earthquake insurance.

STEPS TO TAKE FOR A PARTIAL ALERT
(When an earthquake or aftershocks are expected)

1. Stay out of hazardous places, such as crowded public assemblies, or old, unreinforced brick or concrete buildings.

2. Move your cars out of the garage or carport, and park them on level ground, out in the open.

3. Be sure that cupboard, closet, and refrigerator doors can't swing open. Tape or tie them closed, if necessary.

4. Secure television sets, VCRs, stereos, computers, and other electronic gear. Keep them *unplugged* when not in use.

5. Check supplies and renew if necessary.

6. Put top-heavy and unsecured objects on the floor.

7. Place your earthquake kit by the door from which you will exit. Include warm or waterproof clothing if necessary.

8. Keep pets outside in a fenced yard with a good supply of water.

STEPS TO TAKE FOR A FULL ALERT
(If time permits before evacuation)

1. Complete all steps for a partial alert.
2. Turn off the utilities to avoid damage from fire or water. (This step could be skipped if you remain close by.) Remember that the gas must be turned on only by a gas serviceperson.
3. If you don't have enough drinking water stored, fill plastic containers, seal and store securely.
4. Clear table tops and shelves unless items are secured.
5. Take the shades off lamps, and lay the lamps on the floor wrapped with pillows or blankets. Secure other fragile items in a similar way.
6. If you have a piano, move it away from windows, cover it with blankets, and brace the legs.
7. Go to your safe outdoor refuge with all family members. Take:
   Earthquake kit
   Extra blankets, sleeping bags, tarpaulin
   Extra flashlights, batteries, other light sources
   Additional food, water, can opener, and utensils
   Sanitation supplies
   Camping gear, if available
   Camera, reading material, deck of cards, games, toys

STEPS TO TAKE AFTER AN EARTHQUAKE

1. Check for injuries. Check and protect yourself first; then check others. Stop severe bleeding. Attempt to stabilize critical injuries. Treat for shock. Don't move injured victims unless absolutely necessary. Search building for additional victims.
2. Check for fires and potential fires or explosions. If a fire has started, try to notify the fire department. Extinguish fires immediately if possible. If you smell gas, or observe that your gas lines are damaged, turn off gas at the meter.
3. Assess condition of building. Look for structural damage, chemical spills, water leaks, sparking electrical lines. If necessary, evacuate the building immediately and turn off utilities.
4. After an earthquake that may have caused damage, evacuate all buildings except where immediate evacuation may

hazardous, such as high-rise buildings, or where there is no safe evacuation area, and unless evacuation would be unsafe for individual. Evacuate *all* buildings with structural damage, chemical spills, fires, or other hazards. Take emergency supplies and equipment to prearranged evacuation area.

5. Request assistance for critical needs. If telephones don't work, send someone to the closest police or fire station. If there is time during evacuation, check to see that telephones are hung up. Don't use the phone except for life-threatening emergencies.

6. Administer first aid to minor injuries.

7. Listen to the radio for emergency information and follow official instructions.

8. Check pets cautiously. Keep dogs leashed or in fenced yard.

9. Expect aftershocks. More damage is possible, and it is possible that a damaging earthquake will be followed by a larger quake.

10. Plan emergency shelter. Keep victims warm and dry. Conduct a thorough inspection of building, inside and outside, before re-occupying building.

11. Check supplies of water and food. Possible sources of water: bottled water, liquids in refrigerator, melted ice cubes, canned goods, tea kettle, water heater, toilet tank.

12. Attend to the emotional needs of victims—including your own.

(See Chapter 7, "What To Do Afterwards," for more detailed suggestions on what to do after the earthquake.)

Appendix II

Modified Mercalli Intensity Scale of 1931

The first scale to reflect earthquake intensities was developed by deRossi of Italy and Forel of Switzerland in the 1880s. This scale, with values from I to X, was used for about two decades. A need for a more refined scale increased with the advancement of the science of seismology, and, in 1902, the Italian seismologist Mercalli devised a new scale on a I to XII range. The Mercalli Scale was modified in 1931 by American seismologists, Harry O. Wood and Frank Neumann, to take into account modern structural features:

I. Not felt except by a very few under especially favorable circumstances.

II. Felt only by a few persons at rest, especially on upper floors of buildings. Delicately suspended objects may swing.

III. Felt quite noticeably indoors, especially on upper floors of buildings, but many people do not recognize it as an earthquake. Standing motor cars may rock slightly. Vibration like passing of truck. Duration estimated.

IV. During the day felt indoors by many, outdoors by few. At night some awakened. Dishes, windows, doors disturbed; walls make cracking sound. Sensation like heavy truck striking building. Standing motor cars rocked noticeably.

   V. Felt by nearly everyone; many awakened. Some dishes, windows, etc., broken; a few instances of cracked plaster; unstable objects overturned. Disturbances of trees, poles, and other tall objects sometimes noticed. Pendulum clocks may stop.

  VI. Felt by all, many frightened and run outdoors. Some heavy furniture moved; a few instances of fallen plaster or damaged chimneys. Damage slight.

 VII. Everybody runs outdoors. Damage negligible in building of good design and construction; slight to moderate in well-built ordinary structures; considerable in poorly built or badly designed structures; some chimneys broken. Noticed by persons driving in motor cars.

VIII. Damage slight in specially designed structures; considerable in ordinary substantial buildings, with partial collapse; great in poorly built structures. Panel walls thrown out of frame structure. Fall of chimneys, factory stacks, columns, monuments, walls. Heavy furniture overturned. Sand and mud ejected in small amounts. Changes in well water. Persons driving motor cars disturbed.

  IX. Damage considerable in specially designed structures; well-designed frame structures thrown out of plumb; great in substantial buildings, with partial collapse. Buildings shifted off foundations. Ground cracked conspicuously. Underground pipes broken.

   X. Some well-built wooden structures destroyed; most masonry and frame structures destroyed with foundations; ground badly cracked. Rails bent. Landslides considerable from river banks and steep slopes. Shifted sand and mud. Water splashed, slopped over banks.

  XI. Few, if any, (masonry) structures remain standing. Bridges destroyed. Broad fissures in ground. Underground pipelines completely out of service. Earth slumps and land slips in soft ground. Rails bent greatly.

XII. Damage total. Practically all works of construction are damaged greatly or destroyed. Waves seen on ground surface. Lines of sight and level are distorted. Objects are thrown upward into the air.

The Modified Mercalli intensity scale measures the intensity of an earthquake's effects in a given locality, and is, perhaps, more meaningful to the non-scientist because it is based on actual observations of earthquake effects at specific places. It should be noted that because the data used for assigning intensities can only be obtained from direct firsthand reports, considerable time—weeks or months—is sometimes needed before an intensity map can be assembled for a particular earthquake. While an earthquake has only one Richter Magnitude, it can have many intensities, which generally decrease with distance from the epicenter.

SEISMICITY OF THE UNITEI

110W

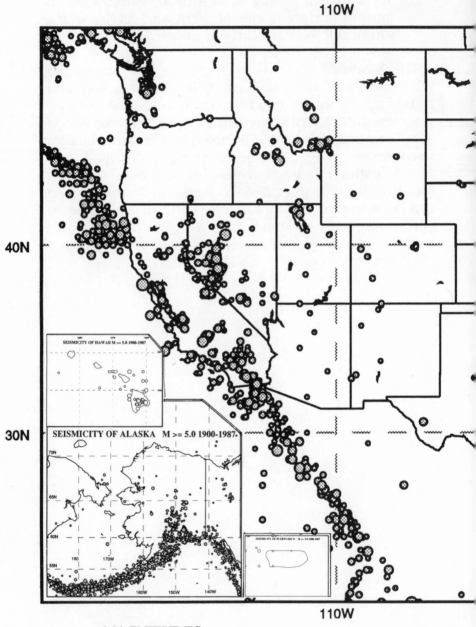

110W

MAGNITUDES

<4.0 •

5.0 ○

6.0 ◉

7.0 ⊛

1667 EARTHQUAKES PLOTTED

NATIONAL GEOPHYSICAL DAT

STATES   M >= 5.0 1900-1987

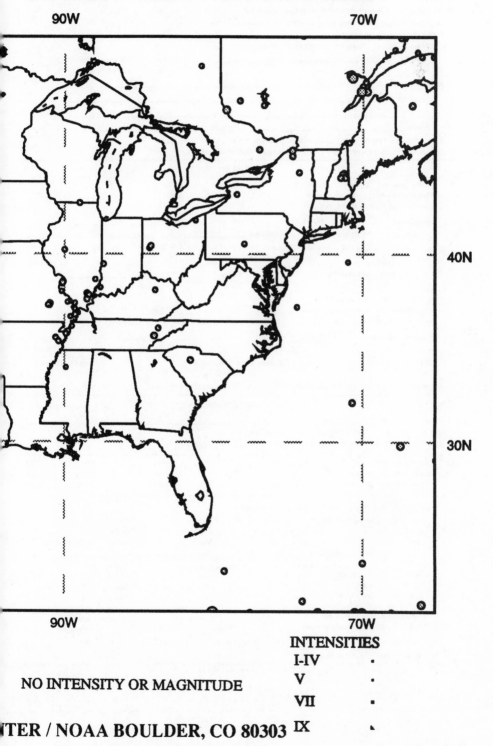

INTENSITIES

I-IV   .

NO INTENSITY OR MAGNITUDE   V   .

VII   ▪

ITER / NOAA BOULDER, CO 80303   IX   ▸

Please answer this questionnaire and return as soon as possible

1. Was an earthquake felt by anyone in your town near the date and time indicated on the opposite page?

☐ No: Please refold and tape for return mail.

☐ Yes: Date _____ Time _____   ☐ AM   ☐ Standard time
                                                                    ☐ PM   ☐ Daylight time

Name of person filling out form _____

Address _____

City _____ County _____

State _____ Zip code _____

If you felt the earthquake, complete the following section. If others felt the earthquake but you did not, skip the personal report and complete the community report.

PERSONAL REPORT

2. Did you personally feel the earthquake?   ☐ Yes   ☐ No
   Were you awakened by the earthquake?   ☐ Yes   ☐ No
   Were you frightened by the earthquake?   ☐ Yes   ☐ No

   Were you at   ☐ Home   ☐ Work   ☐ Other? _____

   Town and zip code of your location at time of earthquake _____

   Check your activity when the earthquake occured:

☐ Walking	☐ Sleeping	☐ Lying down ☐ Standing
☐ Driving (car in motion)	☐ Sitting	☐ Other _____
	☐ Inside or	☐ Outside

   Were you
   If inside, on what floor were you?
   Did you have difficulty in standing or walking   ☐ Yes   ☐ No
   Vibration could be described as   ☐ Light   ☐ Moderate   ☐ Strong

   Was there earth noise?   ☐ No   ☐ Faint   ☐ Moderate   ☐ Loud
   Direction of noise   ☐ North   ☐ South   ☐ East   ☐ West

   Estimated duration of   ☐ Sudden, sharp (less than 10 secs)   ☐ Long (30-60 secs)
   shaking   ☐ Short (10-30 secs)

Continue on to next section which should include personal as well as reported observations.

COMMUNITY REPORT

Town and zip code _____
DO NOT INCLUDE EFFECTS FROM OTHER COMMUNITIES/TOWNS
Check one box for each question that is applicable.

3 a.	The earthquake was felt by	☐ No one	☐ Few	☐ Several	☐ Many	☐ All
b.	This earthquake awakened	☐ No one	☐ Few	☐ Several	☐ Many	☐ All?
c.	This earthquake frightened	☐ No one	☐ Few	☐ Several	☐ Many	☐ All?

4. What indoor physical effects were noted in your community?

Windows, doors, dishes rattled	☐ Slightly	☐ Loudly
Walls creaked	☐ Slightly	☐ Loudly
Building trembled (shook)	☐ Slightly	☐ Moderately ☐ Strongly
Hanging pictures (more than one)	☐ Swung ☐ Out of place	☐ Fallen
Windows ☐ Few cracked	☐ Some broken out	☐ Many broken out
Small objects overturned	☐ Few	☐ Many
Small objects fallen	☐ Few	☐ Many
Glassware/dished broken	☐ Few	☐ Many
Light furniture or small appliances	☐ Overturned	☐ Damaged seriously
Heavy furniture or appliances	☐ Overturned	☐ Damaged seriously
Did hanging objects or doors swing?	☐ Slightly ☐ Moderately	☐ Violently
Can you estimate direction?	☐ North/South ☐ East/West	☐ Other _____
Items thrown from store shelves	☐ Few	☐ Many

Continued on the reverse side

5. Indicate effects of the following types to interior walls if any:

Plater/stucco	☐ Hairline cracks	☐ Large cracks (many)	☐ Fell in large amounts
Dry wall	☐ Hairline cracks	☐ Large cracks (many)	☐ Fell in large amounts

6. What outdoor physical effects were noted in your community?

Trees and bushes shaken	☐ Slightly	☐ Moderately	☐ Strongly
Standing vehicles rocked	☐ Slightly	☐ Moderately	
Moving vehicles rocked	☐ Slightly	☐ Moderately	
Water splashed onto sides of lakes, ponds, swimming pools	☐ Yes	☐ No	
Elevated water tanks	☐ Cracked	☐ Twisted	☐ Fallen (thrown down)
Tombstones	☐ Displaced ☐ Fallen	☐ Cracked	☐ Rotated
Chimneys	☐ Cracked ☐ Broken at roof line	☐ Twisted ☐ Bricks fallen	☐ Fallen
Railroad tracks bent	☐ Slightly	☐ Greatly	
Stone or brick fences/walls	☐ Open cracks	☐ Fallen	☐ Destroyed
Underground pipes	☐ Broken	☐ Out of service	
Highways or streets	☐ Large cracks	☐ Large displacements	
Sidewalks	☐ Large cracks	☐ Large displacements	

7a. Check below any structural damage to buildings.

Foundation	☐ Cracked		☐ Destroyed
Interior walls	☐ Split	☐ Fallen	☐ Separated from ceiling or floor
Exterior walls	☐ Large Cracks		☐ Bulged outward
	☐ Partial collapse		☐ Total collapse

b. What type of construction was the building that showed this damage?

☐ Wood	☐ Stone	☐ Brick veneer	☐ Other _____
☐ Brick	☐ Cinderblock	☐ Reinforced concrete	☐ Mobile home

c. What was the type of ground under the building?

☐ Don't know	☐ Sandy soil	☐ Marshy	☐ Fill
☐ Hard rock	☐ Clay soil	☐ Sandstone, limestone, shale	

d. Was the ground: ☐ Level   ☐ Sloping   ☐ Steep?

e. Check the approximate age of the building:
    ☐ Built before 1945   ☐ Built 1945-65   ☐ Built after 1965

8. Check below any structural damage to

Bridges/Overpasses	☐ Concrete	☐ Wood	☐ Steel	☐ Other
Damage was	☐ Slight	☐ Moderate		☐ Severe
Dams	☐ Concrete	☐ Large earthen		
Damage was	☐ Slight	☐ Moderate		☐ Severe

9. What geologic effects were noted in your community?

Ground cracks	☐ Wet ground	☐ Steep slopes	☐ Dry and level ground
Landslides	☐ Small	☐ Large	
Slumping	☐ River bank	☐ Road fill	☐ Land fill
Were springs or well water disturbed?	☐ Level changed ☐ Muddied	☐ Flow disturbed ☐ Don't know	
Were rivers or lakes changed?	☐ Yes ☐ No	☐ Don't know	

10a. What percentage of buildings were damaged?

Within 2 city blocks of your location	☐ None	☐ Few (about 5%)
	☐ Many (about 50%)	☐ Most (about 75%)
b. In area covered by your zip code	☐ None	☐ Few (about 5%)
	☐ Many (about 50%)	☐ Most (about 75%)

Thank you for your time and information. Refold this card and tape for return mail.

Bibliography

American Red Cross, Los Angeles Chapter. *Earthquake Preparedness Checklist for Business and Industry.* Los Angeles, CA: American Red Cross, Los Angeles Chapter, 1985.

American Red Cross. *Disaster Preparedness for Disabled and Elderly People.* Los Angeles, CA: American Red Cross, Los Angeles Chapter, 1985.

American Red Cross. *Assisting Disabled & Elderly People in Disasters.* Los Angeles, CA: American Red Cross, Los Angeles Chapter, 1985.

Bolt, Bruce A. *Earthquakes.* New York: W.H. Freeman & Co., 1978, 1988.

Booth, Basil, and Fitch, Frank. *Earth Shock.* New York: Walker Publishing Co., 1979.

California Division of Mines and Geology. *California Geology.* Subscriptions: $10.00 per year (12 issues). P.O. Box 2980, Sacramento, CA 95812.

California Legislature: Joint Committee on Seismic Safety, Special Subcommittee. "The San Fernando Earthquake of February 9, 1971 and Public Policy." Sacramento, 1972.

DeNevi, Don. *Earthquakes.* Millbrae, CA: Celestial Arts, 1977.

Federal Emergency Management Agency. *Coping With Children's Reactions to Earthquakes and Other Disasters.* Pamphlet #48, Washington, D.C.: FEMA, 1983.

Federal Emergency Management Agency. *Learning to Live in Earthquake Country—Preparedness for People with Disabilities.* Washington, D.C.: FEMA, 1985.

Gere, James M. and Haresh C. Shah. *Terra Non Firma— Understanding and Preparing for Earthquakes.* Stanford, CA: Stanford Alumni Association, 1984.

Gribbin, John. *This Shaking Earth: Earthquakes, Volcanoes, and Their Impact On Our World.* New York: G.P. Putnam's Sons, 1978.

Margerum, Terry. *We're Not Ready for the Big Quake.* San Francisco: Association of Bay Area Governments, 1980.

National Research Council. *Real Time Earthquake Montoring.* Washington, D.C.: National Academy Press, 1991.

Panel on the Public Policy Implications of Earthquake Prediction. *Earthquake Prediction and Public Policy.* Washington, D.C.: National Academy of Sciences, 1975.

Reitherman, Robert. *Reducing the Risks of Nonstructural Earthquake Damage: A Practical Guide.* Sacramento, CA: California Seismic Safety Commission, 1983.

United States Geological Survey. *Earthquake and Volcanoes.* Washington, D.C.: Superintendent of Documents, U.S. Government Printing Office, Subscriptions: $6.50 per year (6 issues).

United States Geological Survey. *Lessons Learned from the Loma Prieta, California, Earthquake of October 17, 1989.* Washington, D.C.: U.S. Government Printing Office, 1989.

United States Geological Survey. *The Loma Prieta Earthquake of October 17, 1989.* Washington, D.C.: Superintendent of Documents, U.S. Government Printing Office, 1989.

Index